Listening to
People of Hope

Listening to People of Hope

by

Brother Leonard of Taizé

The Pilgrim Press
New York

First published 1984
by A R Mowbray & Co Ltd,
Saint Thomas House, Becket Street,
Oxford, OX1 1SJ

Library of Congress Cataloging in Publication Data

Leonard, of Taizé, Brother, 1940-
  Listening to people of hope.

  1. Christianity—United States. 2. United States—
Description and travel—1981- . 3 Leonard, of
Taizé, Brother, 1940- . I. Title.
BR526.L46   1985   277.3′0828   84-27371
ISBN 0-8298-0544-3 (pbk.)

The Pilgrim Press, 132 West 31 Street, New York, NY 10001

CONTENTS

Litany for a People of Hope   vii

Introduction   1

1. A Mosaic of Living Stones   7
A New West Side Story   7
At a Southern Baptist Business Meeting   13
Cadets, Cambodians, and Charismatics   18
Reaping Souls at the World's Fair in New Orleans   24
"Bread and Roses" in Philadelphia   29

2. Journeying from Suffering to Hope   36
A Life Commitment in California   36
A Car Ride in Chicago   40
A Young French Woman En route to the
    Savages of Louisiana   45
"Death Always Comes Too Soon"   51
Walking to St. Peter's in New York   53

3. People Called to Justice   57
COPS in San Antonio   57
A Black Christ Painted by a Mexican Priest   66
Social Justice in New Orleans: The Main
    Organizing Clusters   68
A Home for Runaways in the Bay Area   73
A Baptist Ministering to Seamen   78

4. Gospel Families   85
New Life Unlimited in a Chicago Ghetto   85
A Couple of Hopeful Presbyterians in San Francisco   91
A Cathedral of Blessing Hands   97
St. Joseph the Worker's Impossible Dreams   100
What Heaven Is Like, Heard in Harlem   107

5. Struggling for a Reconciled Church   **112**
   The Laughter in the Joke at St. John the Divine   112
   Concerts of Prayer at Moody Bible Institute   116
   Listening to a Baptist Sermon   122
   Searching for Roots in California   130
   Twentieth-century Religion in New Orleans   139

6. An Armful of Gifts—New Ministries   **148**
   Nusquama's Interchurch Center   148
   Forms of Suburban-urban Solidarity   151
   An Invisible Structure of Pastoral Care   154
   Turn Your Building into a Village   159
   The Seven Task Forces in Each Parish   163

About Taizé by Brother John of Taizé   **169**

Litany for a People of Hope

(after each invocation a Kyrie Eleison may be sung)

Christ the Lord, you became poor and you offer the kingdom of heaven to the poor of the earth, you fill us with your riches.

O Lord, gentle and humble of heart, you reveal a new world to all who abandon themselves, we receive of your fullness.

O Lord, you fell prostrate on the ground, and you show us a path of consolation in our distress, you are the joy no one can take from us.

O Lord, you shed your blood, and you give the cup of life to seekers after justice, you quench every thirst.

O Risen Lord, you showed yourself to your disciples and you pluck from our flesh our hearts of stone, we shall see you face to face.

O Lord, you divest the powerful and clothe peacemakers in festal robes, you transform us into your likeness.

O Lord, first of the living, you welcome into the kingdom of heaven all who die for you, we dwell in your love.

Introduction

Through these pages I want to celebrate the 'people of the Beatitudes' in North America who struggle, pray, work and hope. This book is also an invitation to readers in every country to involve themselves in the discovery of people who, by their very lives, make visible a future for the Church, to visit with others, ignored or rejected, and to learn to love again the universal life of Christ as the most precious gift in our own existence. This could be seen as a 'spiritual exercise'. It can lead us to a new attitude in life, a life rooted in the Risen Christ who leads us indeed from division to reconciliation, from suffering to hope and from ourselves to the One in whom every being lives and exists.

Before they were written down, these pages were talked over in airports, bus stations and on the train with two other Brothers of Taizé living in New York City during a 'pilgrimage of reconciliation' which we undertook last year in the United States and Canada. One of the goals of the pilgrimage-meetings with people of all ages (especially students and young adults) and all denominations was to search for the roots of peace and reconciliation. The key question that arose each time in those meetings was: how can we become, in each one's own life situation, a force for concrete acts of reconciliation among Christians and in all the situations which tear apart the human family? At the same time, by praying around the Cross, by silence and singing, by a celebration of hope, the meetings were an experience of 'accompanying Christ in His pilgrimage through humanity as the Crucified and Risen Lord', who leads us from suffering to hope.

Being the John the Baptist, I had to go some time before

the pilgrimage started, or started again, to the places where we had been invited. Each time there was of course some organizing involved. For instance, one of the aspects of the pilgrimage weekends was that the participants went out on Saturday afternoon into the area in order to meet with Christians who in one way or another are involved in neighbourhood groups, community organizations and all kinds of ministries, especially among the poor. A committee, sometimes helped by open hearings with many more people, brainstormed around the question: do we know such places of hope here in town? Networks of often hidden signs of hope became visible; they had to be visited and invited to be part of the weekend. In Ames, Iowa, where the first pilgrimage was held, a group managed to find fifty-eight places of hope, all people involved in areas like the nuclear freeze or communication techniques or drug rehabilitation centres or a contemplative house of prayer or a family with a handicapped child. Ideally, this led to neighbourhood meetings on that very weekend, in which the regular participants of the weekend, often living outside of town, could take part and find inspiration. It was meant to be a listening experience: what are *you* doing as a Christian for peace and reconciliation? What are your deepest motivations? What keeps you going? How to persevere? For many, in the preparation as well as during the weekend itself, this was a powerful experience, allowing a completely new approach to what the Church is and where it finds its unity. But to explain this, and other things, to the small crowd of people who had taken the initiative to invite us and who had perhaps expected to get involved in a less time-consuming job, it was necessary to sit in on a lot of meetings and to wait until a spark of recognition started to kindle people's imagination.

During those preparatory visits I was glad not to have to get completely caught up in the anxiety of the committee and to have free time to walk around and see for myself a lot of 'people of hope'. Curiously, as soon as your eyes are open

2

for it, you see them everywhere, and every person you meet, after some reflection will know other ones. Like Diogenes with his lantern, I went through those towns and cities, trying to grasp the gifts given by God to the churches, linking up groups with other groups, neighbourhoods with other neighbourhoods, denominations with other denominations. Where can I see experiences, initiatives that will lead the Churches beyond their present reality? Where are people who anticipate in whatever way the future of the Church and the unity we search for?

People are yearning for hope. Often they are so overwhelmed by the problems that a visitor from outside is almost necessary to reveal the newness of the initiatives they have inaugurated. Sometimes I noticed the fear that the emphasis on hope would prevent a thorough analysis of what is going wrong. I believe the contrary: precisely when situations, seen 'objectively' from a human viewpoint, seem to be hopeless – and the divisions in and among the churches are considered by many as hopeless – the challenge arises even more sharply to become creators of hope as well as revealers of all the signs that point towards a different future. Somehow people are taken very seriously when they start to analyse or to criticize. But optimism should not be confused with hope. Hope is a struggle, a new birth given to people and situations that are always in danger of collapsing. Hope is an act of faith, an action grounded on the certainty of the Resurrection, and of the love that discerns what is right and full of promise.

Our pilgrimage-meetings were held mostly in cities, and this book reflects that fact. There is another reason why cities seem to be privileged in these pages in comparison to the countryside. An extraordinary urbanization continues to take place in the contemporary world. A French subway specialist said recently that by the year 2000 fifty per cent of us all will be urban dwellers. Travelling around, everybody can see the endless blocks and neighbourhoods and urban areas built out of a centre that has lost its centrality. Urban

3

sprawl has led people out of the city to the suburbs and out of the suburbs to exurbia and further and further – subways, trains, highways, cars and planes linking them up – so that the urbanized areas are filled with many more people than the central city itself. Many places in the countryside are invaded, physically and psychologically, by the action radius of the city. Malls, decentralized services, businesses booming at the outskirts of the cities encroach upon the last green pastures. The city is everywhere.

This book consists of thirty stories, gathered in six cities – New York, Philadelphia, Chicago, San Francisco, San Antonio, New Orleans – as well as in one imaginary city. The stories were chosen out of hundreds as examples of a Church becoming here and there what she is called to be: a people of the Beatitudes. A people one yet diverse; suffering yet hoping; uniting struggle for justice and contemplation, seemingly in contradiction with each other but finally found at the heart of the other, 'each begetting the other in a ceaseless exchange'; a people reborn to new relationships of communion, rooted in the gospel; reconciled and reconciling; welcoming God's gifts and giving whatever has been given to them. The stories describe in a bird's-eye view this upcoming but still hidden future of the Church, present already now as a promise.

The first chapter 'A mosaic of living stones' describes the diversity of visions people have of the Church. I ran into so many ecclesiologies that it seems impossible to summarize them in a limited number of types. Each pastor – they still determine pretty much alone in which direction their church will navigate – tries to bring in that little something which translates his or her gifts, education, sensitivity, energy, expectations, often in such a way that other options are excluded. This diversity, however, shows the magnificent creativity the Church is able to awaken from generation to generation; it is as if there is no way to grasp fully the horizon of communion in the human family we usually call church, community, assembly, parish or congregation. I

4

like those visions of the Church *together*, one enriching the other. If they would mutually include the visions of the others, I'm sure the Church in the city would become a beacon of hope. 'Journeying from suffering to hope' tells some moments in the life of people for whom Good Friday and Easter have become the thread which weaves the very fabric of their existence. In New Orleans an Ursuline nun of the eighteenth century became so much alive for me through conversations and readings that she walks in this chapter with the others, in the same communion of saints. 'People called to justice' reports about some grass-roots initiatives on the social and political level. 'Gospel families' lists some parishes and congregations in which I found enough hope to believe that everywhere it is possible to start over and over again, renewing from within what seemed to be empty, old and without life. 'Struggling for a reconciled Church' consists of some reflections about ways in which the churches could achieve reconciliation. I started out with the question how I would be able to reconcile in myself all the different expressions of Church life, how I could make my own heart and understanding more universal. In the last chapter I'm dreaming about new ministries – for every one of us according to the gifts we have received – that could help us to jump the wall of our uncertainties and hesitancies and make us become signs of contradiction, witnesses of the Gospel, creators of hope....

How many things did I omit or did I not even see! Why didn't I report on Madison, San Diego, Minneapolis, St Louis, Miami, Houston...? At least New York, Philadelphia, Chicago, San Francisco, San Antonio and New Orleans do represent completely different worlds, located in the same country but light-years away from one another. Christians do hear sometimes about initiatives around the country but only insofar as their own denomination is concerned, the rest is blank. Frequently I have noticed deep ignorance about the others, in one's own neighbourhood, in the same city or even nationwide. Besides ignorance,

5

stereotyped and clearly out-of-date images are common. There is often just a polite coexistence according to which the clergy will meet for an ecumenical dinner or an occasional ecumenical service. It is very rare to find a passion for the visible unity of the Church beyond one's own denominational dividing lines. Unity is frequently seen as an additional occupation, somewhat of a luxury; it is, moreover, often understood as uniformity, and therefore refused. Many think if there is already a spiritual unity, why bother to come together? But if spiritual unity is a reality, why can't it be expressed in signs of visible unity so that the Church is really one and the world may believe? In Protestantism especially, the search for the unity of the Church often consists only in support for international organizations that speak out about political issues of our time. There is less the awareness that the Church universal is called to witness by its very life, to be a reflection here and now of the communion of the human family brought about by Christ's cross and resurrection.

St John, the contemplative, saw Christ walking among the seven golden lampstands which symbolized the churches of seven cities in Asia Minor. However limited my contemplative gifts may be, I am sure of having glimpsed the silhouette of Christ in the light of the North American candelabra, sure enough to share with you this book of hope.

Taizé, Fourth Sunday of Advent 1983

1

A Mosaic of Living Stones

A new West Side Story

I like being in New York. Everybody, everything is there! Questioning the inhabitants of our block in Hell's Kitchen would be enough to tell you all about the sufferings of the whole world. Crossing Manhattan from east to west at the hour when people are coming out of work is enough to grasp all of the stubborn resurgence of human hope.

The hand raised to call one of those yellow cabs which dance their way along the broken-down avenue, the ear deafened by the disharmony of the humming of buses, planes and subways, eyes blinded by the crowd of faces and furtive glances, the heart transported by the sirens of the great boats on the river, the nose tickled – here by the scent of perfume, there by the smell of drugs – and your feet are killing you from having unknowingly walked along miles of corridors.... Humanity gets lost here, humanity spreads out its wings here.

A while back I made a study of the iconography of the city of Jerusalem, as shown on the capitals of pillars in cathedrals and churches at the time of the Crusades. Jerusalem had suddenly become the obsession of the West, mythologized to the point of becoming overlaid with images of the heavenly Jerusalem. A mythology so strong that every town, church or monastery had to become this same Jerusalem, with the same measurements and the same circularity as the heavenly city. The cities which we love nowadays do not have this sacred signature, are not built around religious values. They are spiritual deserts, and the step we took in going to live on a fifth floor in an infamous district in New York is perhaps not very different from the

7

steps taken by the first hermits of the Church who went into the desert to sit up in the skyscrapers of their day. To want to be a Christian in Manhattan, to however small a degree, is no small thing.

Some years ago I made a thirty-day retreat in Paris. One day the director of the retreat invited me to walk along an avenue of linden trees which overlooks Paris. The theme: contemplation of the Incarnation. 'Here are the Three Divine Persons looking down upon the whole surface of the globe of the universe, filled with people. And seeing all those who were going down to hell, they decided, in their eternity, that the Second Person would become a human being in order to save the human spirit...'.

Paris at 5 o'clock in the evening. Think of all those people, 'some white, others black, some peaceful, others laughing, some in good health, others sick'. Hear 'how they talk with each other, how they swear and blaspheme'. Look at what they do, 'they cheat, they kill, they go to hell, etc'. 'And at the same time what the Divine Persons are doing, they are bringing about the most holy Incarnation' (Saint Ignatius of Loyola, Spritual Exercises, First Day, First contemplation, the Incarnation).

There is a story of the fourth Wise Man who started out late on the road to Bethlehem, and only arrived in Jerusalem for Good Friday. That is a little like what happens to us when we want to witness to Christ in the city: the Incarnation takes on the face of the Passion, and for us, that of compassion.

I looked for an apartment in New York for our community. A strange experience: I was swimming against the current of what everyone else was looking for. Finally, I found an almost condemned building, in which we squatted. On the fifth floor there were two lovely windows; from them we could at least see the sky of New York. The apartment was a disaster, uninhabited for the past year. The hookers who had made their little world here had clearly not done good business. The second attraction of this 'railroad'-

8

style apartment, conceived for Irish immigrants in the nineteenth century, was the roof. Today it looks more like a prison yard than anything else, because of the barbed wire which has had to be put around it, following several burglaries. I climbed up there, thinking again of my experience in Paris, and said to myself: the only possible way to live here is to throw oneself into a life of compassion.

Just recently I had a kind of confirmation of this. I took part in a radio broadcast during the night from Saturday to Sunday. The listeners, many of them young people, could call in with their questions. Right at the end of the programme a young woman asked me: 'Do you really believe that God forgives?' She pressed the point: 'If, for example, a terrible thing happened to me, just a few days before, do you think that there could be forgiveness?' I thought of the awful rape of a nun in East-Harlem, which took place on the same day we were holding a prayer in the cathedral. And also of what a friend to whom I had confided my bewilderment said: 'In New York, you know, we're in competition with the devil'. Is there forgiveness?' This question took hold of me, and I believe that the 'yes' said with all our heart is truly the sine qua non of our presence in New York.

Clinton is a highbrow name for the dirty streets that have always been known as Hell's Kitchen, where for a hundred years successive waves of immigrants have lived in squalid conditions. Only in the last few years pockets of more affluent housing have appeared: here and there one sees other kinds of faces on the block. Next to the majority of Puerto Ricans and Dominicans, the old located in tenements, SRO hotels and the high-rise housing projects overlooking the Hudson, there are now many people between twenty and forty years old – gays and others – searching for alternative lifestyles. They often have a certain intellectual background, but are working as lift operators, doormen, waitresses or messengers; they belong to the generation whose parents left the city in the fifties for the suburbs. Can Clinton keep its character? It's a big issue for the (many) neighbourhood organizations and block associations.

Standing on the roof of our apartment and looking west, you glimpse beyond the five-storey tenements the piers of the harbour, lining up into the Hudson River. To these now-decaying docks, immigrants arrived from all of the world's ports; today cruise ships bring people out of the city for a voyage to nowhere, without any particular destination. Sometimes you hear the ship's horn at their departure, a romantic sound that reminds you all at once that Manhattan is an island. Downtown just beyond Manhattan Plaza, home for many artists, rises the huge recently modernized central bus terminal operated by the Port Authority. People arrive from all parts of the country and land right on 42nd Street. On summer evenings, sitting on the roof, you notice that planes heading north fly exactly above our block between 9th and 10th Avenues. In the distance, the gigantic twin towers of the World Trade Center, suspended in the air. To the east Times Square, the theatres, the New York Times building, and only three blocks away the office towers of midtown Manhattan and Rockefeller Center. Only those which line the Avenue of the Americas are visible, cold monuments of an alien culture for those who live on this side of the world. Uptown is the Lincoln Center for the Performing Arts, built in a neighbourhood of Puerto Ricans who had to leave their homes to make room for this temple of culture dedicated to opera, ballet, plays and concerts.

Characteristic of Clinton is the five-storey red brick tenement. Along either side of Ninth Avenue people live in these overcrowded buildings before moving away, when they can, to a better neighbourhood. On summer evenings, around Ninth Avenue, life explodes as in an African slum: loud music from the transistors fills the air, street vendors ply their wares on every corner, people sit on the stoops talking, drinking beer from paper bags and looking at the passers-by; everybody is walking around, eating, scream-

10

ing, gambling, yelling, dancing, cooking, looking at each other. For many, the borders of Clinton seem to be the end of the world. Puerto Rico, Santo Domingo, Port-au-Prince ... it's all right here.

For many of them, and even more for the tramps and the shopping-bag ladies around Roosevelt Hospital, Clinton is a place of despair, as was Hell's Kitchen, a nowhere wedged between the riches all the other human beings are capable of bringing together, an island of the neglected. Yet where else is it possible to find so many self-help groups, block associations, welcome centres for the elderly, drug rehabilitation centres, food co-ops, houses for mentally disturbed, settlement houses for lower-working-class people, religious groups of all kinds, drop-in centres for runaways, a 'dwelling place' for shopping-bag ladies, tenant associations?

Four brothers of Taizé (five, when I am there) have lived in Clinton since 1978. At that time, along with the '413 W 48th St Residents' Association', we started to fill the twenty apartments in the building with people from the neighbourhood and to legalize our situation through long negotiations with the city. A while back the landlord had found it no longer profitable to care for the building; he let it deteriorate and stopped paying property taxes. When the city took ownership, the tenants tried to get some basic services – heat, hot water, plumbing – all to no avail. Then the last remaining tenants began to have weekly meetings, sometimes – because everything was a crisis – even more than once a week.

I remember, when I arrived and the venture began, only five apartments in the house were occupied. There were Mallory, the super, Jim and Eric, Sophia, Michael Reddy who died later of bone cancer at Roosevelt Hospital, Michael Cortzak who was always sitting on the stoop drinking his beer, Overton T Sackstedder IV and Kathy from St Malachy's Actors Chapel on 49th St: people from every walk of life. At that point the building was physically

11

falling apart, mostly abandoned. Only a few people paid rent to the city, and the city paid nothing in return. The weekly meetings were held at Michael Reddy's bedside amidst the smell of decay and the sight of dead cockroaches falling off the wall. When Michael died, we decided to come together each time in a different apartment. Rather than having officers, the host of the meeting would lead the conversation. In this neighbourhood, where people rarely invite anybody to their homes, this was an important step.

Little by little, a new spirit of resistance and self-affirmation came about. A co-operative endeavour was set up in order to make 413 W 48th St a real home. The tenants paid rent to their own association, enabling them to start basic repairs, helping one apartment after another to get into shape. Painting, plastering, a new entrance door, new windows, a new bell system, work on the boiler that was always broken, complete renovation of several apartments – all became possible with a rent of around 100 dollars a month. The tenants themselves took charge of the building.

Then, in the spring of 1978, the association decided to approach the city more formally. The Department of Receivership evaded its request to turn the management of the building over legally to those who had repaired it. They were threatened with eviction. At the end of 1978, an application for an 'interim lease', involving full accounting of all financial transactions, was submitted to the Commissioner of the Housing Preservation Department. This application led finally to a one-year lease. Long and complex negotiations still had to be pursued, in co-operation with five other buildings in the neighbourhood, under the auspices of the not-for-profit group, Housing Conservation Co-ordinators on Tenth Avenue. The tenants also had to present their case to all the political groups with housing committees in the neighbourhood to seek their approval. Finally, in June 1981, through the Tenant Interim Lease Program, the Board of Estimate voted to sell the building to the association, for 250 dollars per apartment.

One of the brothers, who played a leading role in this process, says that the most important thing in it all was, and is, the spirit in the house: 'There were so many events, really difficult situations, but we went through it together, so that in this unlikely setting there was like a re-creation of village life.' We come together every year at Thanksgiving for a pot-luck dinner, not to talk about 'business', the affairs of the building, but just to be together. Once in a while we rent a van for an outing to Long Island. We have shared a lot of things: from dramatic conflicts between competing block associations to cups of coffee and friendship, from hundreds of emotionally charged issues to robberies, living together like people who live in a small village, in the heart of what the whole world thinks of as an inhuman and dangerous city.

At a Southern Baptist business meeting

Trinity Baptist in San Antonio is a booming church. Descending the hill, I see that the church with its spires is only part of an immense complex. I'm still too early for the appointment with a man who wants to introduce me this evening, a new convert who will meet me in a black Volkswagen at the steps of the church in a little while. While waiting I wander through the complex.

How many things are going on here! I read a list of Sunday school classes for all age groups – birth till walking, the deaf department, marriage up to age 28, single adults aged 56 and over. There is a father-son 'camp-out' planned at Alto Frio Baptist Encampment at Leakey, Texas and a single adult Bible study about the life and times of Elijah. Meat for the wildgame dinner can be taken to the modern frozen-food locker. And the mixed bowling league is hoping to form four to six teams of four people per team. In Eagle Pass they will be doing water-well drilling, growbed food and animal production for world hunger. On Bitters Road they are constructing a Korean Baptist Mission. In Monclo-va, Mexico and in Nigeria, preaching and ophthalmology are

13

planned. At the Halloween costume party, 'come-as-any-thing-or-anyone-but-who-you-are'. It is a city in itself, one could spend the whole day here taking part in the church's activities and forgetting about one's solitude. In the sanctuary the choir is rehearsing on the podium in an amphitheatrical position. Is this a social club – the image many Europeans have of American parish life – where people can chat in moments of boredom, while their children play basketball and some grown-ups hang out on the parking lot? There must be more behind it. All those hundreds of people – many are single, I guess – are walking around in some unknown cloud of happiness; in the twinkling of their eyes I see that part of their dreams – American dreams for sure – have come true, here, on the better side of town where we can solve our problems of stress management, be part of a 'super growth' commission and uplift ourselves in the moving services on Sunday where five thousand people show up and fill the parking lot before marching into the sanctuary where the Spirit is expected to drive in himself.

But here is the Volkswagen. Out of it crawls my guardian, who will be helping me out of my resistances by simply sharing with me and by uncovering both the gifts that are present here and my admiration. We find a place to sit down, in an immense room where five hundred people are eating and chatting. During the meal I have to tell my story at least seven times, not only to my guardian and immediate neighbours but also to the ministers who pass by, a little curious about that strange bird on their branch. We exchange some quick words before their hands reach the next row. The pastor asks me to 'carry greetings to our fellow-babies', which must be a reference to the possible born-again people among my friends. Another minister tells me that they believe in the great commission and adds: '... Jerusalem, Judea, Samaria, and the uttermost part of the world ...'. I must have looked like another Thomas, because he explains that 'we believe San Antonio is our Jerusalem'. 'San Antonio is your Jerusalem?' I ask. 'Well,

14

the twentieth chapter of Matthew says: "Go ye therefore to all the world . . .; ye shall be my witnesses . . ."; Jesus spoke about Judea, Jerusalem, Samaria and the uttermost part of the earth, and that's just as applicable today as it was then, that his church is supposed to go to its Jerusalem, for us San Antonio.' 'Yes, yes, because it's here . . .', I say. 'Judea, you know, is our state, our Texas, Samaria the United States of America, the outermost part of the earth, foreign mission.'

But now the pastor, after having shaken hands, told his witty jokes to the newcomers, made his compliments to the ladies, advances slowly towards the microphone and asks us to allow him to intrude on our evening. Five hundred people eating with knife and fork makes a tremendous noise indeed. He has a high pitched voice and stands there, sure of his ascendancy over the crowd, visibly amused and good-humoured, swinging his glasses from time to time through the space around the small pulpit and getting them back on the tip of his nose as soon as he has to look over his notes. He has that quality of elegance and ease that make some ministers perfect masters of ceremonies. Some announcements about the choir that has to grow to two hundred people; presentation of the new members and guests (I have to stand up), and then he asks for prayer-requests. A hush falls over the room and several people stand up. A lady tells about a girl of seventeen she happened to meet, who has medical problems, is afraid and suspicious, and says that she does not believe in God. It is a solemn moment, where the pastor hears the concerns that are expressed, repeats them over the microphone and gives them back to a layperson who has to sum it all up in a prayer. This whole prayer sequence expels the social entertainment atmosphere and prepares for a spiritual word that the pastor will now speak before the business meeting starts.

As soon as he begins to speak, there is an electrifying concentration. All stop whatever they were thinking and listen. The lights in the big room are dimmed and only one spotlight falls on the person of the pastor. First he compares the people who are gathered in the room to the early disciples in the Book of Acts who were designating offerings, selecting people for leadership, delegating responsibilities to people. Then he wants to throw out an idea he has on his mind. He is asking if 'one or two or fifty' – and they don't have to sign up on a piece of paper or to talk about it to him or anybody, 'it's between you and the Lord' – could get up on Sundays thirty minutes earlier. One member of a family, perhaps two, maybe some are already doing it. The Lord has blessed this church, he says, last year. They have seen more people than ever. They want to give to God the glory. Thirty minutes earlier to spend in prayer for the ministry of the Church on that day.... Before coming to church, pray, specifically for the preaching of the Gospel, wherever it is preached, and for the invitation extended to the people. 'Just pray.'

Angels pass. A tender ray of light rests in the eyes of the people who have somehow, in the midst of the struggles and disillusionments of their lives – which is not only the fate of the poor – kept intact the purity of desire, that attractiveness deep down in them for the fulfilment of all human life in the Kingdom of God. A time out of time for him.

But eternity is for later. I stay another moment. They talk about a contract of almost a million dollars for new construction in the complex of buildings two blocks south for single adults. They want to start a parking building and other constructions costing several million dollars, because they anticipate continuing to reach more and more people. Before they get into the details, my guardian and I take off, we want to talk.

Children are playing around us as we sit outside the church on the ground. It is cooler now, at this exquisite hour of the day. My 'guardian', as I call him, tells me about himself. His parents were fervent Baptists and belonged to a hard-core wing. The preacher shouted a lot and the child felt frightened. Hell was depicted with the most sinister instincts. At the age of six or seven the child begged his

16

parents to let him go to Sunday school rather than to church. All his first recollections of the church are definitely unpleasant. As a teenager he felt a tremendous pressure from his parents to become a born-again, but he resisted this, rebellious as he had become against the Church, although he felt guilty especially of not becoming a minister. But his mother and her friends didn't give up at all and assured him that they would be praying for him and that one day he would surely make the right decision. He found that awful, that kind of persecution. One Sunday morning, one of his friends walked down the aisle to become a born-again. He thought: 'This is my chance. Let's get this over with. They won't bother me any more' and he went down the same way. He was born again. This was his religious conversion experience. He became a nominal Baptist in high school, but at college he dropped everything. Of course, he kept some religious residues in him, some sense of a deity, he says, and the willingness to lead 'a moral life'.

Later his mother recommended a church in San Antonio. In order to satisfy her wish, he went there at least once, with an assumed name so as to avoid the insisting letters you get automatically for years as soon as you imprudently leave your name and address on a piece of paper with Baptists, and then there are all the other efforts to get you back there in the pews. In the meantime he had experienced episodic depressions and after having followed different treatments with mixed results, he was struck by a few words in a cheap booklet he had found in some bookstore, saying that depression is based on spiritual alienation. One day after that he woke up and said to himself: 'Why wouldn't I pray? Why wouldn't I ask the Father, the Son and the Spirit to come in and to become part of my life?' And it was, he says, as if a stone that was laying on his whole being was taken away. He has felt relieved since then. After his depression cleared up – his voice is trembling tonight though, and my first impression of him was an impression of fear, the fear of tumbling again into that hell of helplessness which is called

17

depression – he wanted to join a church. He had a lot of sympathy for the Catholic Church, but said to himself that he had started out as a Baptist and it would therefore make sense to become one again. He came to Trinity Baptist. On a Sunday afternoon he was baptized again, by total immersion, as a symbol of his conversion.

I'm surprised by the soberness and simplicity of his story. No extravagances, except perhaps for the sometimes extravagant suffering he must have gone through. I'm sure there are thousands of Baptists who have known the same situation at home, renounced at church and rediscovered later that ineffaceable seal in the soul which reveals in a sudden clarity the very meaning of our existence, filling us with joy.

His Volkswagen drives me to the West Side. On the corner of the street kids have stolen the cash at the HEB and police officers are standing behind the broken windows. Back in my room I feel renewed and nourished. Yes, underneath all the struggles and the panic of human desolation a birth is at hand. Don't wait indefinitely. Give up what keeps you astray. Don't settle down in a chimera of doubts. Is He not the Risen One who opens the gates of heaven in every person you meet, in every oppression you see people immersed in? Are we not, with the poor and the meek in San Antonio, that 'Jerusalem' of the Baptists, called to belong to the People of the Resurrection?

Cadets, Cambodians and Charismatics
The only thing I know about Evanston, north of Chicago, is that a World Council of Churches assembly was held here in 1954. Because I am early, I walk around aimlessly. On one block I see a van filled with uniformed people, like a police unit, stop at a warehouse. I'm intrigued so I follow them, and discover that this warehouse, where cars were repainted before it went bankrupt, is the Reba Fellowship Church, the very place where I wanted to go. The people in uniform have caps on with red circular bands reading 'Salvation

18

Army'. Men and women, cadets from their training school, who as part of their formation visit a different Christian church every Sunday. They all seem to be broad-shouldered people in their uniforms, with a look of idealism and spiritual energy glimmering in their bright eyes. Later, looking down from the top row of the amphitheatre, they give me the impression of a group of penguins on pilgrimage, getting themselves ready for the people to take a picture. Obviously, they don't know the style of congregational dance, bell songs and inspirational witness that prevails here; with their tight uniforms they must be used to a more structured form of worship. But when we are asked to sing 'Mighty fortress', they rise from their seats.

On the left some Cambodians from the uptown area are sitting, constantly receiving explanations from an Episcopal priest who is a member of the Fellowship, a small group leader, celebrant of the daily communion services and in charge of the newly converted. I regretted that the Cambodians didn't get more attention from the assembly, for instance by a reading of the Gospel in their language.

Every three months the whole Fellowship takes a week for rest and renewal, one full week without meetings. The leader asks what people did instead: wrapping Christmas gifts, time with the children, walking in the streets, visiting friends, swimming, going out for dinner, a party until midnight, a mystery story on TV. And now it is possible to fly again with 'eagle's wings'. Normally the worship takes two hours with times of quiet, a play from Scripture, teaching and a free sharing. This Sunday the service is particularly unstructured. The leader is standing in front of a large white sheet hanging from the ceiling, as a banner that says 'Christ has died, Christ has risen, Christ will come again'. There are hundreds of people, and many of them are young adults or young families. I like the invitation to 'spend some time in praising the Lord', the alternating currents of silent prayer and common singing, the dance for the children in which many older people join, the freely

19

charismatic atmosphere of praying with body and soul, in manifold expressions. A handicapped woman reads the magnificent verses of St Paul about the splendour of the heavenly bodies and the resurrection of the dead, when a young couple announced the death of a woman twenty-seven years old who had been ill for seven months and who was baptized two weeks ago. The leader prays with the young people, and I feel a deep oneness among us all resounding in me. 'What rises is incorruptible. Weakness is sown, a strength rises up'.

Among a certain number of members of the Reba Place Fellowship there is financial sharing. At lunch, in one of the households – we are twelve around the table – we speak together about this extreme sign of common belonging, expressed by people of different ages. It is a gesture oriented towards giving a witness, living a simple life style and being willing to put all the material goods apart from your own ownership, dedicating them to the Lord. The effect of it is that no one is any richer than anyone else in material goods. They 'lay down' all their possessions and use them in common. It is a free decision made by those who belong to 'the communal sector' of the Fellowship. The other members can of course live a simple existence too, but they don't take the commitment of a common purse. Individual needs have to be talked about, discerned by small groups and the three stewards who oversee the financial decisions concerning things like paying for college or buying a new car. There is also a vacation guideline. The stewards help people decide what trip to take and how much money it is appropriate to spend. People are allowed to go beyond a three hundred mile radius to visit their family every other year. They make an exception of course, when there is a special need. The risk of having some members involved in financial sharing is that it might create a difference between an inner and outer circle. That temptation exists until they are able to see themselves as part of a big circle, the Church, and to see the financial sharing as a special calling that doesn't make them better Christians or give them a greater belonging in 'the Lord's family'.

I noticed at the worship service the important role given to leaders. And over lunch everybody remained silent until the woman who was presiding started the conversation, asking one or the other to introduce themselves or me to speak. During the first part of the meal we did not speak, it was time to eat; only in the second part was there an ordered conversation. The advantage is that you don't get lost in a noisy and superficial atmosphere, supposedly natural and spontaneous but in reality empty chatter. The meal becomes a celebration in which one is attentive to the others, revealing them in their uniqueness, open to all; it becomes a common creation. I noticed the struggle of some who restrained their reactions while still trying to remain spontaneous and relaxed. As a group they wait for someone to lead them. It reminds me of monastic obedience. There is a sense of leading and following, they are accountable to someone as well as to each another; nobody wants to push him or herself and therefore there has to be an enabler or a servant who reveals the others to themselves and to one another and who in the final analysis is in charge of the unity between everyone. This attitude is part of their desire for consensus, for real unanimity. They don't like to make decisions that not everyone feels right about. Often the process of making a decision will take a very long time. They want to wait for their brothers and sisters either to come with them or perhaps to let them understand that they are wrong or to discover that there is another way to do something that nobody has thought of. It is basically an attitude of waiting to be led by another than themselves, expecting that they will be in unity when 'the Lord's leading' comes.

I am interested to see a fellowship that traces its roots back to the sixteenth century Anabaptists discovering the laws of common life as it is expressed in orders and congregations in other denominations. They don't want to see themselves too strongly as an order, because like the Anabaptists they are reluctant to build up groups of people who could give the impression of being more dedicated or holy than the others. They see the Church as one group of disciples of the Lord, composed of people who are called to do different things. My opinion is that affiliation with the Anabaptists drives them to a continuously renewed search for perfection. The Anabaptists separated from the Catholic Church in order to pursue the creation of a perfect church, and this legacy remains as a residual temptation. Anyone who claims this legacy will have to struggle so as not to repeat the same process of separation from the others on the way to an always unattainable perfection. It is therefore interesting to see the Reba Place Fellowship resisting this propensity and refusing delineations – for instance around the question of financial sharing – that would be divisive rather than unifying. On the other hand, because they don't have a vision of the unity of the Church they claim to have the full life of the Church, to be a new Church. An order for them would be a group of people who would not have the full life of the Church all to themselves. They don't see themselves as having been given any specific ministry; they claim the totality of Church life. In spite of this, some members have felt the necessity of committing themselves financially in a more radical way than the others, taking the risk of creating a separation within the congregation. Another example of the risk of purism is the group of people who left because of their refusal of the interdiction to remarry – and because of other problems as well – and who founded Christ Church, also in Evanston.

The people who originated the Fellowship in 1957 were all Mennonite seminarians who started out as a Mennonite Voluntary Service unit and who ended up in creating 'a church with a common life'. Some years ago they decided to affiliate themselves with two denominations, the Church of the Brethren and the Mennonite Church. Most of the people were of one or the other origin, therefore they chose both rather than to pick one above the other. The Catholics, Episcopalians and other Protestants of various kinds, if they want to join the Fellowship, can't remain a member of the churches they came from.

The members of the Fellowship live in the same area, within walking distance of one another, so that they can meet in other members' homes and pray together during the week. The Fellowship is divided into small groups, fourteen or fifteen in all. Pastorally it is easier to relate to a smaller group, to get to know each other and to share their lives in a deep way with each other. It is a kind of decentralization meant to foster the unit of the whole congregation. Each small group has a leader or two, and each small group leader has an elder supervising him or her. All the small group leaders meet with the six elders on Monday night. The elders know therefore exactly what is going on, the individual pastoral problems as well as the issues that are coming up. This whole structure is not new: Wesley set up similar things for the Methodists in England, some Latin American Pentecostal churches are doing this, the Hernhuters (Moravians) had similar structures at least in the past. It is all part of the search for common life, for accountability, for a church that does not function only on Sunday but the whole week long, in which the whole person is involved. One also thinks of the total commitment of the original Jerusalem community. A person's life is really with his or her brothers and sisters, open to them and laid down for them, in every way. This includes mutual spiritual direction and a ministry of healing with intensive counselling.

The Fellowship is located in South East Evanston. There are some very poor people in the area and many are on welfare. The rent is in general high, so there is a lot of moving in and out, especially in the apartment buildings. The Fellowship members promised the neighbourhood when they bought apartment buildings that they would not fill them up with white people but keep them integrated. One of the members tried to find ways of buying a building or a couple of buildings for the Cambodians who, having discovered Christ in the refugee camps or having been baptized in the Reba Place Fellowship, have become Christians. In Uptown they are living on a lower financial level than the other members, which is in contradiction to the option of the Fellowship for a similar life style for all. But it is not certain that this will work out, because the Cambodians want to live in Uptown where there are more Cambodians. Also, they are thinking about ... starting their own church.

Reaping souls at the World's Fair in New Orleans
The First Assembly of God on Airline Highway has no direct fellowship with the Catholic Charismatics, but the staff people tell me that many Catholic Charismatics take part in their church, in the worship and in union-type programmes like a Holy Spirit Conference or a Harvest Festival. They do everything, they say, to maintain fellowship with those Christians who are both in and out of the Catholic Charismatic communities and of the Assembly of God. But they are not necessarily involved with them in terms of speaking at their churches or promoting their work. I have noticed this attitude often in pentecostal, evangelical, fundamentalist circles: Catholics are welcome in so far as they accept our positions and enjoy our services, but there is no reciprocity. The First Assembly of God doesn't need it, they have lots of people (six thousand they say) and lots of ministries that keep them busy. There are a hundred and ten actively operating home Bible study programmes that meet weekly in people's homes, congregating in small cells. Fifty or sixty more are in training. The Bible-study home cell groups have a set curriculum, a set time, a set teacher. 'It's Koinonia.' It is a time of study of the Bible, a time of prayer and of ministry to the particular needs that someone may have. So the church is decentralized during the week throughout the entire metropolitan area. They also have an ongoing training programme

in order to teach the teachers. The small cells are called to be evangelistic, firstly by inviting neighbours and relatives, secondly by channelling into these home cells people who 'got an experience of the Lord' at the Sunday services or during crusades. The home cell groups also serve as a channel to communicate announcements about services, special meetings, sessions, retreats, seminars.

There is a tremendously active TV ministry. Their satellite reaches all over the country. At the end of the morning, late at night, on Sunday night their minister speaks and speaks. For young people, especially for drug addicts, they operate a Dave Wilkerson-style Teen Challenge Programme with three components: a coffee house/drop-in centre on Burgundy Street, open night and day, that ministers to people in the streets, a crisis centre for people who really want to change and who make a commitment, where they can stay for fourteen to thirty days, and after having been screened that way, if they give the indication of wanting to be rehabilitated and to be reintegrated in the community, there is a barn to welcome them to the north of the lake with space for thirty-four residents who stay there for sixteen to eighteen months. It is a faith ministry and nobody has to pay tuition. They call it a full rehabilitation process. Proudly they say that eighty-six per cent of those who leave never return to their former life. In the building on Airline Highway they also have a total education programme with a fully credited private day school for 550 students from K (Kindergarten) through to 12th grade. There is also a day-care centre for seventy to ninety children. Walking through the building I see lots of offices, a printing shop, a TV production centre for the daily TV programmes out of the sanctuary. The rest of the TV ministry staff has a building in Metairie, in which the computer is housed as well for the internal administrative book keeping, mailing lists, correspondence. In the future they hope to open a place where girls on the streets or in social dilemmas as a result of abuse or promiscuity would find a home. I see a school where men and women are training for full-time ministry.

At the centre of this church stands a Reverend from Arkansas who received the call to turn New Orleans from a Sodom to a Nineveh. With that Southern puritanical attitude so different from the spirit of New Orleans, he finds the place 'a centre for lusty, worldly pursuits, filled with free-wheeling passion and sin'. 'New Orleans is a party town, flesh pot, sin centre, drug den, perversion pit, gambling capital, crime arena, and stronghold of Satan.' What would he say of Amsterdam? What gradation in his vocabulary would he find to describe our neighbourhood in New York? Would he speak in the same style about economic exploitation? Would he feel 'the very powers of Satan' walking on Wall Street or in his own Metairie, simply in comparing people's privileges with those of others who live in the housing projects? One day with his wife he walks in the French Quarter; in the narrow streets 'the very presence of evil seemed to hang just above our heads'. His heart 'hurt so bad' seeing the frightened or weary looks, eyes were 'glazed and fixed'; 'high-pitched laughing, shouts of confusion, the muffled mutter of a thousand meaningless conversations all flowed together in a cacophony of disillusionment and desperation'. It was as if he saw sin itself 'as an octopus of monstrous proportions'. It was enough reason for him to accept the call from the First Assembly of God (located at first on Elysian Fields Avenue) and to start to save the city with the hundred people sitting in the pews who had not even yet received the baptism of the Holy Spirit. 'Was New Orleans a Sodom, so wicked it was in danger of fiery destruction? Or was it a Nineveh, a great city waiting to turn to God when the Lord's messenger was willing to "preach unto it the preaching that I bid thee"?'

Since then the Reverend has been speaking in ten or fifteen commitments a week, at five Sunday services, a miracle rally on Monday night with prayer for the sick – eighty per cent of those attending belong to other churches

– the regular midweek service on Wednesday evening, and then all the TV and radio speeches as well as executive responsibilities on the level of the General Council of the Assemblies of God. Although I have brought up no criticisms at all in the conversation – it only bothers me that Catholics can't find in their own churches that happiness they experience here – the staff people emphasize that they are not interested in kingdom building, in an 'empire' or a 'dynasty'. All their outreach is for the Kingdom. They say that they have certainly put as many people in other churches as they have in their own. They have reproduced a congregation the size of their own in other churches, not only in Assemblies of God but in other denominations as well – and they mean the Catholic Church. The Reverend certainly is one of those men who because of their charismatic gifts and drive are capable of motivating people like the staff people I talk with, giving them a real desire to do whatever it takes to promote their church and the cause of Christ wherever it will be accepted, reached and received, even beyond their own denomination.

They suppose that I have heard criticisms against the Reverend's personality, but it is not true. I noticed some feeling of competition, Catholics reacting like cats that put out their claws or on the contrary rounding their backs in seemingly serene nonchalance. Elsewhere pastors envy the direct, uncomplicated missionary consciousness of the Reverend who wants 'to take the city for God'. In a certain sense the style of spirituality practised on Airline Highway, the enthusiasm, the emotiveness, the shouting and the witnessing, the belief in the devil and in the 'Jesus factor' fits somehow sociologically in New Orleans' overall extravagance. I have no doubts about the unselfishness of the Reverend, his caring attitude for the needy and his mercy. But the staff people insist. One says that he was surprised to see the kind of house the Reverend lives in. Someone of his status, experience and success should be living in some very big estate, but no, he lives among the common people in the 'normal' suburban setting, in Metairie. People seem to have criticized him for the car he drove but he didn't own that car, it was given to him. People blessed through his ministry give things and that is normal, they think. Accepting gifts doesn't mean that somebody wouldn't be a person of sacrifice. One of the disparities they want to be reconciled with in the evangelization efforts through TV is the fact that a certain image is projected on you; people suppose certain things about a person's life style that are not at all consistent with the way the person really is. If you work next to him, if you feel the pulse of the man, if you are around, you are able to appreciate his attitude of sacrifice. People do it with all TV personalities. It is true, the Reverend doesn't live in poverty, but his life style is only consistent with his needs.

Four years ago the Reverend laid out a five-year plan. This year is a year of 'saturation', which means that they want to saturate the New Orleans metropolitan area with the Gospel. Last year the focus was on family involvement, their training, their commitment, getting them equipped. This year is the year of harvest, the year of reaping souls at the World's Fair. Millions of people will be in New Orleans whom otherwise the city would never see. Then another five-year projection subsequent to the World's Fair will follow. They want to give every child in every housing project a knowledge of what the Gospel is about, and some ray of hope, the only way of hope being the Gospel of Jesus Christ. In the First Assembly of God one finds an unrelenting evangelical thrust in order literally to cover the city and reach every individual. If all the people in New Orleans went to church on Sunday, they say, the churches – and there are many – would hold only fifty per cent; there would be more people than church seats to fill! 'The harvest field is out there.' The aim is not to build this unit on Airline Highway but to bring everybody to a decision, to expose them to the Gospel.

And now the social implications. Once you bring people to a decision, once they reach that experience of salvation within their heart they will bring about social change. Invariably you see an upgrading in their life style, because you see the infusion of the life of the Spirit. It doesn't mean that everybody becomes a millionaire. But there is an attitudinal shift, the persons look at themselves and their environment differently. Biases, prejudices and stereotypes fall aside. There is an inner change which finds its outworking in self-esteem, self-respect, confidence which 'affects industry, tourism ...'. The Reverend is in a certain way a social rehabilitator, because with the 'Jesus factor' you are like a little leaven in the Kingdom. The staff people tell me that they sometimes hear the criticism that they are not involved on the front lines in social issues but they find that they deal with the basic problem of the individual, which has to do with his own self-respect and deliverance from his own pattern of guilt and condemnation to where he feels in peace about himself so that he can make social changes. They don't want to be isolationists or to put their head in the sand, they are very much behind these social things but the change of the heart, the change in the nature of the individual comes first. That will then bring about in a natural flow a lot of other things, 'we have proven that by thousands of lives'. Jesus did the same thing with the girl, he just told her everything about her past in which she was caught up, about her self-defeating and self-destructive life style, and he wanted her to know him and the 'everlasting life'. The girl brought the whole city to him. The message is: change your life. As soon as the 'sin-problem' in a person's life has found a solution, it has the effect of elevating the person. One's whole existence has to be centred on the 'Jesus factor' after people often have tried everything else. They have to have a change of heart.

'Bread and Roses' in Philadelphia
At a large intersection in downtown Philadelphia, there used to be a Lutheran church called Messiah Lutheran. The pastor was a well-known speaker. The Lutherans would

gather early on Easter morning in large numbers so that the whole street had to be closed off. The young boy, who was maybe thirteen or fourteen, had gone to early Mass. His mother was very careful about the house and wanted it especially perfect for Easter, but she had forgotten the front window. So when the young boy returned from church his mother told him to go out and to clean the front window: he didn't like to do it but he did. While he was up the ladder washing the window, the sunrise service ended and crowds of people came walking down the street where the young boy was working. One man was very keyed up from the sunrise service; when he saw the young boy there working on Easter, he shouted up at him: 'How dare you do this on Easter day!' The event left a very deep impression on the young man's mind.

That young boy is now the pastor of St Elizabeth's Roman Catholic church, a small parish in a totally black neighbourhood, located in an area of evident and pressing human need, with sad blocks of abandoned houses. There is need for hope. At least on Easter morning, the day of the Resurrection, the day of celebration of what is at the heart of all humanity's future, people of this neighbourhood come together in a sunrise service, allowing them to rediscover their deepest roots together. The Catholics are involved in this because a Monsignor always has the feeling that the man of his youth, if he was still alive somewhere, would come back and would see that the young boy had understood. . . .

Previously, the priest worked in the diocesan office, which had required him to articulate a lot of teachings of the Church and of Vatican II. One option stood out very clearly since Paul VI's encyclical about the development of peoples: anything that can help people to be more human is properly a work of the Church. That is the basis for him. Even though it is on a small scale in a neighbourhood parish, the same philosophy and the same conviction can be put to work. A school already existed for many, many years. His idea was, if possible, to create a service arm of the Church which would be so strong, in personnel and in visibility, using the church property, that people would be able to sense in seeing the church that this is not just a place to come to worship or to go to school, it is a 'church-in-service'. There was no blueprint. He simply responded to what was coming from the people. As a matter of fact, a month after he arrived, there was a budget crisis in the State which meant that people who depended on public assistance were receiving nothing. A day later, the first day of July (he had come the first week of June) the street was filled with people coming to the rectory for food. Clearly, because of the crisis in the government, there was nothing artificial either in the people begging for food or in the church organizing help. On that boiling hot day and for ten straight days, they did nothing else from morning till night than unpacking and handing out food to the people. There was a strong sign that the church had to be involved in food, and the theologian in the pastor made the link, theologically and spiritually, with the Eucharist. The first thing they did was to use an empty space in the lower church where much junk had accumulated and to begin an emergency food programme.

Later the parish organized a counselling service for children. The parish didn't want the church to be dominant in the neighbourhood but to be part of it. They opened up the church facilities for meetings and community gatherings. In these meetings the question of housing frequently came up. They discovered that in the whole neighbourhood there was no group working to fix up people's homes despite the fact that the government was coming up with a programme. So the 'service arm of the church' took on that programme and contracted with the city. It has to do with homeowners who are older and who have a fixed income, with the vast amount of vacant homes and the cost to try to renovate them; the idea was to try to keep at least the homes in which the older people lived viable. For a small amount of money it was possible to make sure that the roof and the heating and the electricity and the plumbing was working, which helped the older people to make the house look good and could incite others around to make their house nicer. Another time they heard of a programme for pregnant women and discovered that it operated through government funds available to supermarkets: women received a voucher to get basic nutritional food. They found out that the programme did not function in their neighbourhood, even though it had the highest concentration of poor people. The priest went to the Health Department, and asked if the service centre could become the supermarket, as the only non-store in the whole country licensed for this programme.

The pastor believes in Church membership. The service centre that helps people with housing, with fuel, with counselling and teaching the children, with the school, is necessary. But compared with all those things church membership is the single thing that makes the most difference in people's lives, because it is not just a physical need. Once they are members of the church, people change, their outlook changes, their feeling about themselves, their attitude towards the neighbours. 'I really believe it, although I don't diminish our other efforts but across the board, looking at it, the greatest gift I believe that could happen to the poor people in North Philadelphia is to become church people', to belong to Christ in community with others. It changes the way an individual looks at him– or herself. That doesn't happen in one day, of course. But the pastor has seen it. He has seen people come with hostility and bitterness and over a period of time, in church and with all that church means, meeting other people, watching talented people, praying, singing, working on actions that affect the neighbourhood, they became free of hostility and impressed the others with their simple, strong and clear faith and hope in spite of all the hardships of life. Constantly there is bad news but they keep going on.

Monsignor has become less optimistic than when he read

32

Teilhard de Chardin in the seminary as a theology profes-sor; he is closer to a Lutheran approach of separation between the Gospel, the Church and the struggle in the world. His enthusiasm for a change in political structures has gone bankrupt. His desire to be involved with political activism has lessened. He prefers to concentrate on social help, hoping that the recipients will become part of the church. He has no wavering, no doubt, no hesitation that the parish has to have a preferential concern for the poor, he is 'deeply, simply' convinced about that. But working on the structures leads to a dead end, he thinks.

There was a phone call from '222', the diocesan building, saying that an African Cardinal will come for a visit. I suppose the Monsignors over there needed to take a nap and dispatched the Cardinal and his staff to see the grassroots of the Church's presence among the blacks. We have to organize ourselves quickly, to arrange our ecclesiastical clothes and to line up on the sidewalk. I had met the Cardinal some years ago in Africa, and he has remained the same smiling figure I had seen celebrating in Mathare Valley among thousands of slum children, on the edge of Nairobi. We give him flowers (meanwhile the sidewalk has filled up with some curious bystanders from the area), and a tour of the community service centre. Sisters give a brief explana-tion: the emergency food distribution programme, the housing programme, the programme for pregnant women, the community store, the roller-skating programme that provides part-time employment for youth, the resources and referral service, the food buying club, the office that delivers dinners to elderly homebound, the early learning programme, the counselling service, the clinical medical assistance, the CYO activities. The Cardinal seems im-pressed, a photograph is taken, and he heads back to '222' in his car.

A Korean Sister had told about her art ministry in the parish. She is part of the shared ministry of the clergy and Sisters who every day have the Eucharist together, gathering visibly around the altar as a symbol of their participation in the ministry of the Lord. At one moment I see her in the basement working with a class on ceramics, later she meets at the entrance with the men's club as co-ordinator for the senior citizens putting out beer and corn, at Mass she will lead the singing, this evening she has a prayer group and only in between does she do her own work, weaving, embroidering, designing mosaics or stained glass windows according to the orders she receives from churches. Her bishop had hoped that she would come back to Korea with a whole convent of Missionary Sisters of the Precious Blood but the Sisters already have plenty of missions in Africa and don't want to start other ones for the moment. So 'I got stuck here'. It is very interesting that a parish of poor people allows itself this luxury of hiring an artist in order to beautify life. And she likes to be in this parish, among the poor people who are culturally deprived and 'who need beauty'. She tells me that she has received that tremendous gift which is the gift of human relations – certainly the African Cardinal thought the same thing when the Sister explained to him the life of the parish – 'I discover more and more deeply that we bring Christ to the other through human relationships'. Being present in a prayerful way with the poor people, she is growing deeper into the love of God because of their faith. They are teaching her more than she can teach them. And as a young Sister she needs this constant communication and presence in the parish. One day when she is forty or fifty she hopes to be more mature and then be able to create the masterpiece of her life, the most beautiful painting ever made. She runs away, she has to be available to everybody.

After lunch one day, we talked in the rectory about St Elizabeth of Thuringen after whom the church is named. She was born at the beginning of the thirteenth century in the Hungarian royal family; she married Ludwig IV who reigned over Thuringen and Hessen and whose throne stood on the Wartburg (in what today is Eastern Germany).

Around 1225 terrible famines and epidemics raged in many of the German provinces. Her husband was away for a diplomatic mission that the Emperor had asked him to accomplish. Elizabeth, certainly influenced by the Franciscan movement and the whole mystique of poverty of that time, decided to give all the provisions of the year, the corn, the barley as well as her own jewels, to the poor whom she welcomed in a house at the foot of the Wartburg castle. Ludwig's counsellors were furious to see their master's riches disappear. It seems that Ludwig himself was very understanding on his return, without perhaps knowing how deep the sources were from which his wife's attention to the poor came, and how far it would lead her after his departure as crusader and his death. Anyhow, in the Franciscan legendary stories of the thirteenth century and in Giotto's paintings in the chapel Bardi of the Santa Croce in Florence, we find a touching story that later was taken over elsewhere in Italy and in Germany in literature and art. It became famous in the nineteenth century under the title 'The miracle of the roses'. The story goes that Ludwig, returning home from a hunting party, sees his wife with a big basket in her hand. Angry that she would give bread to the poor, he approaches her but when he comes closer he discovers roses instead of bread in the basket. The team at St Elizabeth tells me that they would like to share with the poor of their neighbourhood 'bread and roses', just like St Elizabeth. I tell them that Luther, kidnapped after his trial and confession before the Emperor in Worms, was brought in secret to the same Wartburg in 1521. He took the pseudonym of Knight George and, in spite of terrible solitude, worked there, on his 'Patmos' as he said, on the first German translation of the New Testament.

2

Journeying from Suffering to Hope

A life commitment in California
Her family has lived in Oakland since the 1800s. She has the same blue-blue eyes as her uncle and godfather, who is guardian of the international Franciscan curia in Rome. More Franciscan priests are part of the family, and her parish is also manned by Franciscans. By the time she got to college, she had the feeling she had to be Catholic but she couldn't yet. She said to herself: 'I hear these things in the Gospel, I hear these things at Mass but what does it mean to me in terms of a life style?' In spite of all her Franciscan background she found no answer until she ran into the Catholic Worker movement. For her, seeing the life in the Worker houses was an instant conversion-type experience: 'My goodness, look at this, it's been around for forty-some years and I never heard a word about it and it's exactly what I'm looking for'. In that instant she found an answer that has never changed since then. Rather than simply following her family's beliefs, at nineteen she discovered on her own what she wanted to do and what she wanted to be.

At first her family grimaced, but they quickly became supportive. Four years have passed, and she thinks she has mellowed from a certain self-righteousness and a 'this-is-the-only-way' attitude. The most important thing for her in the Gospel is that we are called to love, to love each other, ourselves, God. How do we know what that means? We know from our experience what it means to love someone; when we love someone we don't want to see him or her hungry or without a home or sad; we are sad when they are sad and happy when they are. Love can take different forms in people's lives, but she thinks that being a Christian has been watered down in this country to the point where it doesn't mean a whole lot any more. Anybody can say 'I'm a Christian' but it has to mean something, to be translated into the reality of existence. For her this meaning has to do with questions like the wealth of this country at the expense of the rest of the world, with taking a stand against the arms race, against investing in weapons to wipe out the world. 'We are called to be uncomfortable in the United States in 1983.' She wants to struggle all the time to overcome boundaries and obstacles that need to fall down, without ever settling down: 'You miss the boat if you think you have it figured out'. Four years ago, at nineteen, she was really into radicality. 'I'll give my coat. I'll give this, I'll give my food, I'll do anything.' But now she thinks she was too absolute because she selected only some parts of the Gospel, and she sees the danger, for the Catholic Worker as well as for Jerry Falwell, to focus on certain things to the exclusion of what others have discerned.

After her tour to New York, Los Angeles and a few other places she came to Oakland and started alone in some storefronts on East 14th St and 50th Avenue a neighbourhood at-cost food store, a free medical clinic, two houses of hospitality and a playground for the kids of families who move into this skid row area, mostly Hispanics. The Los Angeles' Catholic Worker is a very large operation, with eight hundred to a thousand people a day to be cared for and many projects. New York is big as well, but across the country the typical Worker house would probably be a seven- or eight-bedroom house where people live in community, with some form of hospitality, a soup kitchen, a news letter, gatherings and political resistance initiatives. When she came back to Oakland and started a house, she found people very receptive although not ready to take on a commitment. Oakland seems to be one of those cities where social justice people run from one place to another, where just a few people are doing everything. But she specifically wanted a community that was going to do hospitality, resistance, praying together, living simply. She found it hard to find people who were interested in making a commitment to that. She thinks that this reluctance reflects her generation in this country, a generation with no real sense of what it means to be committed to something.

The Bartimaeus community in Oakland is an inspiration to her. She has known them for a long time, six or seven years, and they are still there, committed to each other. She thinks that the Catholic Worker communities should model themselves after groups like Bartimaeus and ask for at least a one-year commitment. How can you build up a community when there is no commitment? One needs at least a year to scratch the surface of one another and to learn to live together among people who have all received the individualistic imprint of our culture. Only when people are ready to move beyond the phase where all the little things disturb them, does one really have something to work from. In her generation people move a lot, divorce, go their own way after a while but she feels she wants to commit her life to this community in Oakland, whatever form that will take. She sees that as essential for her, even if she doesn't find many other people who are willing to say the same thing: 'This is where I want to put my life in terms of how I'm going to act out my values'.

She lives in the back of a house. The place looks like a neglected cloister in u-form. She knew some Franciscan sisters who rented there a few years ago. So she walked in and said: what a perfect place for a community. The place became available, and then the house across the way, and then the other apartment at the front of the house. She lives with some people she knew from years ago. They didn't make a specific commitment to each other but they have a common history. One had introduced her to the Catholic Worker. Another was a room-mate in college, together they used to dream things. Her friend planned to become a physician's assistant, and now she is one of the main people working at the clinic. In Los Angeles the clinic costs the

Catholic Worker only a hundred dollars a month because all the labour is donated, the doctors and the nurses work for free, drugs are obtained at cost. They are bringing about a change in the skid-row area of Los Angeles with a pre-natal centre for women and kids, open four days a week in an area of high infant mortality. Recently, the Oakland group decided one service they could collectively provide was blood-pressure screening. It is all in the beginning stages. A network of friends is already emerging.

Before finding this location, she had looked around in West Oakland. Traditionally Catholic Workers get a place that is run down for a few thousand dollars and fix it up, with labour and supplies donated, but the Bay Area has the highest housing cost in the country, and as she was looking for a place the costs were tripling. A lot of Victorian homes close to the Bay Bridge have been renovated, making the area an up-and-coming neighbourhood so that the people who lived there can't rent any more and have to leave. Oakland has a strong grassroots neighbourhood organization that grew out of the open training institute led by Jesuits. The group goes into the neighbourhoods, invites people to say what they want, for instance to put up stop signs or to clean up the vacant lots or to obtain re-zoning. They empower people, making them conscious of their right to protest and to intervene. Church and community people work together in this organization.

How does she keep going? She has three part-time jobs, the community is not yet solid, the projects are still just beginning, the telephone rings all the time. She is part of a support group of people who all live in the same area, Franciscans involved in social justice areas and in the peace movement, some Sisters and the Catholic Worker people. It is 'crazy' trying to figure out all their schedules. To share their lives they meet every couple of weeks, trying to build an extended community. They eat together, have some prayer together and every once in a while go away for a weekend. If they are there.... One Sister is in Rome, another is off to a refugee camp in Honduras, back in New York, then off to France, others are involved in a million other groups. Whenever a different group is started in Oakland in any of the areas concerned with the poor and peace, all the same people come: a small world. But how refreshing to hear about all this bustle, how refreshing above all to see a young person pursuing with perseverance the dream of a community with the poor!

A car ride in Chicago
I had attended a rather relaxed parish council meeting at Wellington Avenue United Church of Christ. Upwardly mobile young professionals led the evening, discussing congregational issues in infinite detail, while laughing a lot. I was looking at my watch, because I had promised to spend the evening with a group of street people gathered around the Franciscan Fathers in the Uptown neighbourhood. The parish council had put aside one agenda item, the one for which I had come, for the second part of the evening.

While eating from the potluck that was spread out in wonderful colours on the table at the other side of the room, I was mumbling to myself regrets that I couldn't hear the black man who was going to ask the parish council this evening to support his candidacy for the ministry in the UCC. But then a solution was found, the congregational concerns would take even more time and so the black man could give me a ride to the other appointment. I had never seen such a black black. He was dressed in extremely tight jeans, wore an open shirt and looked like Yul Brynner in *The King and I*. As soon as we were in the car he told me in quick tempo the story of his life.

Along with eleven brothers and sisters, he was raised in a ghetto on Chicago's West Side. His mother made sure that he attended church until he was thirteen years old. But he quickly began to resent the Church and all it stood for. More than anyone else, it was the preacher he resented most. Hearing him often preach sinners into hell eventually

40

became more than he could bear. He left the Church. It was not too long before he took to the streets and began a life of crime and addiction. By the time he was seventeen, he had been sent to St Charles School for Boys and the Chicago Parental School three times each. He was in trouble so much that long before he was seventeen a Juvenile Court Judge had declared that he was incorrigible.

By the time he was eighteen, he was an established criminal and alcoholic. At this point in his life, he hated all forms of religion, and society in general. Hardly a weekend went by that he was not in jail. He had no respect for the law. In his opinion, it was the same as the Church: a big sham. When he drank too much, his behaviour was such that he was often locked up for his own safety. If he was not stealing to buy booze, he was involved in fights. His anti-social behaviour caused him to spend many days and nights in Cook County Jail and the House of Correction. Each time, his poor mother would plead with him to give up drinking and to return to the Church. But he wanted to have nothing to do with religion. At the age of twenty-two, in a raging, drunken blackout, he shot a man during a robbery. He was convicted of assault with intent to commit murder, and sentenced to five to fifteen years in Stateville Penitentiary.

After five years he was paroled to the custody of his parents. His uncle got a job for him in a foundry. The pay was good and it kept him away from his old drinking habits. He married a girl he had known as a child. But his old drinking habits came back; within two years he was separated from his wife and child, out of a job and living most of the time on the streets. Deeply hurt by all this, he drank even more. His poor mother tried desperately to get him involved with the Church, but he didn't want anything to do with it.

Like many chronic alcoholics, he eventually found his way to West Madison Street's Skid Row. For over two years, he was lost in that jungle. All of his time, except

41

when asleep or in jail, was spent drinking or searching for a drink. There are many missions in Madison Street for derelicts, but his distaste for religion was such that he preferred to eat his meals on the streets, and sleep in cars or abandoned buildings. On one of his drunken tours, he somehow ended up in his old neighbourhood. It was dark, and he walked past one of the many storefront churches and went inside. He was drunk and fell asleep. He was awakened by the minister, who told him the service was over. Afterwards, every time he started drinking, he would wake up in a church.

One day his mother saw him drinking in the alley behind her house. She pleaded with him to seek treatment. He told his mother that he had been everywhere and that nobody would accept him. She told him that one of his boyhood friends was the director of a Mental Health facility in the community. She showed him a brochure. He went to please his mother. His friend made some phone calls and got him into Martha Washington Hospital's Alcoholism Programme. There he met a wealthy woman. When she introduced herself, he was still in an awful state of withdrawal and didn't want to be bothered. He especially didn't want to be bothered by an alcoholic patient. She started asking questions of all kinds. He tried to get rid of her by telling her terrible things about himself. But she said he shouldn't put himself down. When it was time for him to be discharged, she gave him her phone number and said to call her if he ever needed help.

He stayed sober for a while, but it did not last very long. He had an argument with his mother and he used it as an excuse to get drunk. Once he recalled the woman's promise and tried to find her phone number in his pocket. But a bottle came along and he forgot about calling her. Later that night, sitting in a gin-mill, he wanted to call her again. Having no money any more, he called collect. He still remembers how good he felt when he heard her voice, even if he was intoxicated at the time. He had figured that she

42

would hang up when she realized that he was drunk, but she didn't. Every time he apologized for being drunk, she dismissed it. He told her that he needed money, a hundred dollars. She promised to bring it the next day. When she arrived the next day, he went with her across the street into a civilized bar. He ordered booze and she had a coke. They talked for a long time. At no point did she criticize him. She kept telling him that he was a good person and that God was working in his life. Afterwards, he went to meet her husband and children. Not long afterwards he was in trouble again. Now he wanted to stop drinking and needed someone to talk to. He didn't want to call Alcoholics Anonymous, so he called this woman again. He told her he wanted treatment. She made some calls and got him in one of the Salvation Army programmes. It was a long-term programme and he stayed there for five months. When he left the programme, the woman's husband arranged a job interview for him at Chicago Federation of Settlements and he was hired as a Job Corps recruiter.

At that time he met his present wife. Even though he didn't care for the Salvation Army's captain, he had often returned to the church there to see old friends and to listen to the hymns. His wife worshipped at Wellington Avenue United Church of Christ and invited him; they joined the church together. His wife was involved in a Mental Health Centre in Uptown and she suggested that he apply for a position in the alcoholism unit. After a year or so with the Federation of Settlements, he was hired at the Mental Health Centre as a crisis worker. At the same time he spoke to the church about involving them in helping him start a programme for derelicts. In 1974 he started this; it was called 'Centre for Street People'. While following an adult education programme and earning at the age of thirty-five his high-school diploma, he began to realize that his work with derelicts was a ministry. He thought of entering the ordained ministry. But he didn't have a college degree, which was required by the seminary. Finally he was admitted to Garrett Evangelical Seminary as a Special Student. During his studies he experienced great pain in his stomach and right side and there were times when he couldn't hold food down. But he was determined to finish the seminary. In 1981 he graduated from Garrett. He buried the thought of the ministry, because he was too concerned about his health. While working full time again at the Centre, he woke up one morning in such pain that he could hardly breathe. In the emergency room at the hospital they thought first he had contracted hepatitis but in December 1981 it was discovered that he was suffering from cancer of the stomach which had spread to his liver. It was terminal.

He felt he had already suffered enough. But he wanted to overcome his anger and affliction and thought that in his life no matter how tough things had been he had always come out of it. By the end of January 1982 he was back to work full time. He believes that he will be healed.

And now he is asking for the ordained ministry. He believes that God has called him throughout his work at the Centre for Street People, through the mouths also of homeless and alcoholic people, through the encouragement of ministers also who referred to his work as a ministry. His life of poverty, his lack of formal education, the crime, his sickness and finally the threat of death made him know that nothing is more powerful than God. He rejects any spiritualization of Christ, he knows that Christ lives within him. 'To spiritualize Christ is to deprive Him of His humanity, but worse still, it is to deprive humanity of Christ.' He believes in the oneness of creation. We focus on worldly possessions and self-preservation, we fail to realize that the only real self-preservation lies in the preservation of all humanity. He believes that we are co-creators, that we can choose to follow Christ or we can choose to follow our own self-interest. 'To bear witness to God's love is not easy; in fact, it is downright hard. As fragile and broken persons, we are continually looking for an easy way out.' He believes in the sacrament of Holy Communion. The drinking and eating of Christ's blood and flesh is an invitation to live out the suffering and struggles of Jesus Christ. When we partake of the blood and flesh of Christ, we are in Christ and Christ is in us. To him, more than anything else, it is a sacrament of compassion, of love for those who are counted among the least of us.

He has since died, being ordained in the hospital, shortly before his death.

A young French woman en route to the savages of Louisiana

Bienville's mother and sister had been educated by the Ursulines in Quebec and so he wanted to have some religious ladies of France in the swampy New Orleans he just had founded. The Jesuit he sent to France for inquiry had relatives who had been educated by the same nuns. I look at Father de Beaubois in a fascinating painting called 'Landing of the Ursulines, 1727' in the Ursuline Convent on State Street. In reality he had not been able to welcome the arriving sisters who disembarked at an early hour when only a few people were at the port. After five months of voyage, a voyage which ordinarily took three months, twelve women from France walked into New Orleans to have 'a very beautiful breakfast' with the Jesuit and his friends. On the painting the Jesuit graciously indicates the direction to go to the ten first New Orleans Ursulines. There are also two postulants, one on her knees caring for one of the blacks, one standing back with her tall hat brought from France; both of these postulants, Claude Massy and Anne Frances, returned to France after some time; they did not have the vocation. Some Indians are around with a baby. A black is sitting on some logs. Palm trees give shade to the Sisters. They landed right at the Mississippi river, so we see a ship. In reality *la Gironde* stopped in the Gulf of Mexico, a hundred miles away, because it couldn't come up the river. The nuns had to travel in sloops and pirogues all day for a whole week and to sleep every evening on the land after

45

having put up mosquito nets. Behind the ship the other side of the river, uninhabited, is visible. The postulant has an open basket and is offering something to eat. Everybody stands still briefly for the picture, and then off they go. Marie-Madeleine, the novice from Rouen, must have been a very joyful person; here she stands in the middle of the painting with her white veil.

At that time, New Orleans possessed only a dozen buildings. The Sisters had been told that a convent stood ready, but it took seven years to build it on Chartres Street. Before it was ready four nuns including the Superior, Marie Tranchepain de St Augustin, had died in the deadly climate. The first Ursulines had volunteered to be sent out by the mother community – at that time there were nine thousand Ursulines in France – because Father de Beaubois had asked them to take care of the military hospital and to start a school. They kept the hospital for fifty years. They opened a boarding school, a day school and they gave classes for black and Indian women and girls. In 1729, after the slaughter by the Natchez Indians, they took the orphans. They also housed fallen women during the first years. The King gave them all the land from Royal Street to the river. When the city grew and expanded and the population increased, the city wanted to cut streets through their property but the nuns loved the enclosure and didn't like to go back and forth out on the streets. In order to be enclosed again the nuns moved to a convent on Dauphine Street which doesn't exist anymore.

I'm in the modern convent, looking through a huge book in which year after year the deliberations of the council have been written down. The first page, written in French, states that all the religious of the monastery of Sainte Ursule of Louisiana met on 1 January 1727 in the infirmary room of the Ursuline convent in Hennebon in Brittany, for the installation of the Superior, confirmed by the Bishop of Quebec. That same month, Marie-Madeleine Hachard received her habit of religion and the name of St Stanislas.

She had left Rouen 'with dry eyes and even with joy' in spite of the 'great grief' she suffered at the last moments, on her pilgrimage of faith to that faraway country 'for which I sigh as I do for the Promised Land'. In Paris she had to wait because the vessel that would take the nuns from l'Orient was not yet in a condition to sail. This was not so easy for her, impatient as she was to leave and to start this incredible venture. She says of herself that she had a happy disposition; each time a difficulty arises she is depressed for a moment but then she discovers something else and turns to that. Waiting in Paris she feels 'tempted in that earthly paradise', a temptation 'of the most delicate kind', and to leave is not easy but 'one must obey'.

The group of religious went to l'Orient by way of Brittany. At Versailles they visit the Palace of the King for some tourism. 'I often had the desire to close my eyes to mortify myself – this kind of mortification still costs me a great deal.' Underway a Cavalier wanted to join the coach, even when he was told that the nuns kept three hours of silence morning and evening. He was courteous and arranged that the nuns' luggage would not be opened at the custom house. It gave them also a feeling of security perhaps; coaches were often robbed along the way. Sometimes the roads were so bad that the coach was completely mired; finding no houses around, the nuns simply sat on the ground. 'We were covered with mud up to our ears, the veils of our two Mothers were splattered with little white spots which gave them a very funny look.' Marie-Madelaine writes to her father who is Procurator in Charge of Accounts in Rouen: 'During this voyage, my dear Father, one laughs at everything. . . . You certainly never expected your daughter would one day arouse the curiosity of whole cities!' Just before Rennes they dine at the Inn with some Capuchin Fathers but 'all we could get was a milk soup, an omelette, and some trifles for dessert'. 'Yet if we spent little, we laughed the more – we were always in a good humour.' From Hennebon the whole group travels with the ferry to l'Orient. The Jesuit Fathers who will embark with them take a carpenter on board as well as a locksmith and several other workmen. 'As for us, my dear Father, please do not be scandalized at this, but we are taking with us a Moor to wait on us' and also 'a very pretty little cat who also wishes to be in our Community, supposing apparently that in Louisiana as in France, there will be mice and rats.' There had been some rumours in Rouen that Marie-Madeleine had not really left and that she had frequently been seen, which makes her think of St Francis Xavier who found himself often in several places at the same time. 'I, however, my dear Father, am not a great enough Saint to manage such a similar miracle'. At the port the nuns meet some Jesuits who are leaving for Pondichery in India and want to take half of the Ursulines with them, without success. A great number of sheep and five hundred chickens are led onto their ship. A Jesuit teases the nuns that they will be put two by two in a sack and the men will hoist them up as they do a bale with a pulley. And now, 22 February 1727, she leaves France for ever and is separated from her father whom she asks not to forget 'a daughter who will remain all her life, my very dear Father, your daughter and servant'.

In New Orleans Marie-Madeleine got a letter from her father posted 6 April and received 20 October. Her sister is now a postulant and she wonders if she will receive the same vocation for Louisiana. Elizabeth is in the same convent. She wishes that her brother would become a Jesuit. 'I am a little angry with my brother because he has not yet written to me. If he lacks a pen ... I shall send him one, or, if it is that he has forgotten how to write, I beg him to relearn it quickly.' The name of another sister is Dorothy. She has a brother who is religious. It seems he was opposed to her leaving, 'many people have considered our project as foolishness'. Her father had bought two large maps of the state of Mississippi – the name Louisiana given by La Salle after the King of France later became the definite name –

but couldn't find New Orleans on them. She sends her father a package on 27 October with the *Prince de Conty* 'which has brought us Negroes from Guinea'; the package contains the account of her voyage on *la Gironde*.

She had told him in another letter that out of any ten ships meeting the same difficulties, not another would have escaped. The nuns had a cabin in the between-decks, eighteen feet in length and seven or eight in width. Six beds were placed on each side, three one above the other, with Marie-Madeleine – the lightest – on top. Number thirteen slept in the passage. They slept in shifts because only two or three could fit in the cabin. The cabin was like an oven because of the extreme heat. At l'Orient the vessel hit a rock twice. The winds were entirely against them. Dinner placed on the table rolled over the tablecloth, and 'we had enough to do just trying to hold ourselves together'. The strong storms and the violent ocean killed forty-nine sheep and many chickens. The nuns were reduced to eating 'rice cooked in water, salted beef and bacon so bad that we could not eat it, and beans seasoned with lard', since they had no butter. They were limited to one half pint of water a day. The wind drove them to Madeira, where the Jesuits visited them. 'Some of those Fathers wore large glasses on their noses in the Portuguese manner and I noticed a young one who took his off to read something – which to us seemed most extraordinary.' The Portuguese Jesuits also wore their hair shorter than the French. The students of the Jesuits all carrying beads to make them look devout, the Intendant of the City and other gentlemen came to see them; the Ursulines remained cloistered on their ship in spite of the pressing invitations by the abbess of the order of Sainte Claire, a Portuguese princess. Later they met 'a Pirate Ship from the Barbary Coast' but finally it withdrew. A lot of dissipation on the ship among the crew was a grief for the nuns. Another enemy ship showed up but withdrew later. The sea again became violent obliging them 'to hang on to something' all the time.

Finally the group arrived in Santo Domingo where they discovered 'Messieurs the Maringouins' and their bites. The nuns wanted to disembark in order to take care of their linens which they wanted to have bleached. Two gentlemen of the Company of the Indies offered them dinner at their home along with a young Creole lady 'who was in no way different from a Parisian – the best-bred Parisian, at that'. The Governor invited them on the same day that there had been a light earthquake. They looked around on the island and the Governor wished Ursulines would come to stay on his island. Marie-Madeleine about her vocation: 'If people only knew the pleasure it is to burn with such a fire (for the salvation of souls), they would ardently desire to be consumed.' Contrary winds and three pirate ships, other winds in the Gulf of Mexico pushed them to the island 'White', and there their ship ran aground. The vessel had sunk about five feet into the sand. Cannons, the ballast and the passenger' chests were unloaded but at the last minute the captain preferred to throw over all the sugar, sixty-one barrels of brandy, other ballast and iron. And then they set sail again, relieved they didn't have to disembark among the savages who 'eat the Whites'. But the ship hit bottom a second time, and death was near. Marie-Madeleine never lost her humour because, making a vow, she noticed that each nun did this privately: 'We were in such a state of trouble and alarm that we could not have all agreed to which Saint we should have commended ourselves'. They had run short of water when finally they were again underway, they anchored at different islands and arrived finally at Belize, at the entrance of the Mississippi river. From there they travelled in sloops and pirogues to New Orleans, which took them seven long days.

I like what she writes after her first year in New Orleans: 'Religion seems to present to our eyes nothing but thorns, but after having experienced them, these thorns are changed into roses'.

'Death always comes too soon'
The houses on the West Side of San Antonio have replaced the old shacks without gas or hot water and with the toilets outside. But Mr Pecina's bed fills almost the whole room of the new house. His wife, two daughters and I are squeezed around his bed where he is sleeping, ill for so long. The gangrene has made his hands black like coal. Mr Pecina is ninety-five years old. He came from Mexico, was an American soldier in World War I in France, got married in Elmendorf, on the outskirts of San Antonio, to a woman whose ancestors came from the Canary Islands, worked on construction of the highways and has now arrived at the gates of death. With the family I'm talking about the widening of Guadalupe Street, the planned clean-up of the corrupted spots around, about the project to make Our Lady of Guadalupe into a sanctuary like the one in Mexico City. But we keep our eyes on Mr Pecina. In between they are saying how long it takes to die. Mr Pecina is not suffering; exhausted, he sleeps, with one tooth over his underlip. Sometimes he comes to and speaks, in an unintelligible way. But it is as if another language deep inside of us speaks between us. The mother has understood that she should give me a present, and I received two of his most beautiful handkerchiefs.

All of a sudden, Mr Pecina, conscious, rises up in his bed and the family says I should pray. It is not sufficient to pray within myself. Mr Pecina's hand is strong, he holds mine as if he wants to tell me that this is the only thing that matters in the whole world, to pray, to pray. While I pray, he looks into my eyes with the innocence of a child. In the language of the Spirit he tells me that he does not know what is happening to him, that there is so much anxiety in him, that the only thing to do is to pray. And I say that although it is perhaps just out of sight for him, I see God coming to rescue him, that God's eyes are already upon him, that we thank him for all, that everything is forgiven and that peace from now on will pervade his anxiety and restlessness. Then, sleep takes him in again, with his black hands spread out on the immaculate sheets. With the family I look at old photographs and I promise to come back at the end of the week.

I take a bus to the Mexican-American Cultural Centre. Every year they organize a Mass for the anointing of the sick, where representatives of all the San Antonio parishes, all old people, are invited. There will be crowds. The bus driver calls out to me when we arrive at W French. I discover that, although MACC is on W French, it is still miles and miles away. I had taken this bus without thinking about directions, because I'm still talking with Mr Pecina inside of myself. But I have to be at this celebration. Finally I get there, just at the end of the celebration. I look for people with tape recorders. An Asian-looking priest or seminarian has taped the music. Happily I find a young Polish Salvatorian. At the offertory people brought not only wine and bread, but also a rosary as a symbol of their prayer, a can as a sign of the problems of old people and a family picture in order to show that old people are the keystones of the family. The bishop explained the sacrament. It is not for dying people – 'don't call the priest, I don't want to die' – it is for life. It gives you the ability to get well, strength for your soul and spirit, more energy, the Holy Spirit. He talked about his mother (the Polish priest, who is far from home, inadvertently says the Polish word for mother) who he had asked, 'aren't you afraid to die?' She said, 'Son, you are priest and bishop, and they didn't teach you that to die is a privilege? Why not? To die is to see the Lord, to see Christ face to face. I am looking forward to it. It is a privilege.' So the bishop said to the old people, 'You are the most privileged people among us all. You have more experience than we do. You teach us, not geography or languages, you teach us the most wonderful thing, you teach us hope. Many of your dreams have come true, marriage, family, many other things. You don't want to go, now, to the beach in Florida, do you? You are looking for something else. You teach hope and hope is in front of you. We learn from you.' He told about a visit he made to a deaf old lady to administer the sacrament of anointing. But she thought, having finally made out the word sacrament, that it was for a marriage and asked, 'With whom?' The bishop said, 'Now I'm going to anoint you, but don't ask me "with whom?" Please stay at your places, we as priests, we want to serve you, you deserve our service. We will bring you communion and we will anoint you there where you are. We are honoured to serve you. You teach us how to live, how to have hope, how to have the vision of eternity.'

At the end of the week I return to Mr Pecina's house. The house looks closed. After having knocked at the door for a long time, a lady speaks to me from behind the door, saying that Mr Pecina has died, but that Mrs Pecina does not know it yet, because they don't dare to tell her, instead they have told her that he is at the hospital. The funeral home will be open until 10 pm this evening. After evening prayer I go to the funeral home downtown. In a very large room like a church I see Mr Pecina lying in state, always with one tooth over his underlip, the American flag – in honour of the soldier – over the casket. His two daughters are there. 'No matter how old your father dies, it is always too soon', she says, and we cry. It is 15 October, the birthday of my own father who died this very year.

Walking to St Peter's in New York
Setting out for the noon prayer at St Peter's Lutheran on Lexington Avenue, another brother and I left the house a bit early and immersed ourselves in the human sea moving up and down the avenues. Impossible to follow a straight course! You have to navigate and constantly negotiate your passage, with the risk of being crushed by the waves of people moving in the opposite direction. Nothing happens as long as you let yourself be carried forward like a boat by the undulating movements of the crowd, all the while keeping up a constant speed, and dodging the Scylla and Charybdis that

surrounds you – ahead, behind, to the left and right. Dreamers, strollers, the headstrong and the timid, beware!

We run into a man who, all alone, is talking to a garbage can, rummaging for pint bottles with a few drops still in them. I look at him, and all the dimensions of his life appear in a flash before my eyes, like the icon of a downhill slide. He's coming out of the Playhouse Theatre, from the three steps entrance under the awning where derelicts meet under the poster of 'The Loss of Roses'. Behind him stands a tree swathed in bandages; it seems to be held up by a chain coming from a second-floor window, like a drunk on the arm of a friend. Trees that contemplated the happy world somewhere upstate were summoned some years ago and must now expose themselves to the breath of life on 48th St, giving shade to the parked theatre limousines and these derelicts on the sidewalks of life. Still higher up, geraniums adorn the fire escapes, embellishing the bars on the windows. Further on, a grass-green carpet lies in front of a big SRO hotel, opposite the recording studio where John Lennon was coming home from the night he was killed. A black woman is standing on the carpet, today's sole representative of the New York Bible Mission Church that meets right here in the storefront. To the right a man is eating his lunch, naked to the waist, above the shoeshine booth, looking upon the immaculate Korean-run market on the corner of Eighth Avenue. No loitering, no visitors, no rooms for rent, no trespassers .... The man in front of the Playhouse Theatre, that icon of a life, continues his lonely conversation. Before the 'Walk' sign comes on, I still have time to think 'Poor man, with your odour of decay, you too the child of a lesser God, I would fear you interrupting my walk, talking to me, telling me the story of your life under the awning of the Playhouse Theatre'.

But the light changes, and all at once I'm among 'the oui girls' as they advertise themselves in big letters blinking in neon, surrounded by an onslaught of electricity. High up you can read the date, the hour, the second and the tenth of

54

a second to remind you of a time of love. This is Broadway, where the word 'love' is shimmering off every single building, as far as you can see and feel, filling for a moment the space of your thoughts and imagination. In a tenth of a second, underway to St Peter's, in the cacophony of the Broadway outbursts of love, I hear Jesus asking deep within me, 'Do you love me, in the wounds and sorrows of the human family?' I enter St Patrick's Cathedral and an atmosphere of prayer lifts me up. As at every hour of the day, a crowd of people is praying, more visible, I think than in many of the world's cathedrals, plagued by the overflowing masses of tourists who invade the place shooting pictures of the architecture from every angle in a desperate attempt to grasp the elusive presence they are unconsciously longing for.

St Peter's Church looks like a prehistoric menhir marooned in the midst of Manhattan, a little pyramid dwarfed by the commercial buildings that surround it. I remember an experience two years ago, on a windy but clear October evening, walking with hundreds of people behind the cross from St Patrick's to St Peter's, praying outdoors and indoors, going from the darkness into the light cast by the majestic three-dimensional Jerusalem cross candle stands. The pews pushed aside, stubby white candles lighting every corner of the church from below street level to five floors above, kneeling on pink, green and blue-checked cushions laid on the floor – a moment of grace for us pilgrims in New York, willing to pray on the floor, at the heart of the city.

'No midday prayer today. Sorry', says the priest. 'I waited five minutes. Nobody showed up.' I look for words to console him, but can't find them because I'm thinking about the evenings I myself waited anxiously for people to pray with us. I should have told him that many people pray in the streets, waiting for the lights to change, standing in line, entering the subway station. And on Ash Wednesday don't you see people's foreheads smudged by the black sign of Lent, revealing something of the inner search alive in many?

A twenty-minute walk back, and we sit down in our own chapel, on the fourth floor, for a delayed midday prayer. We read that story of Jesus asking Peter 'Do you love me?' He asks him three times, as many times as Peter denied him. Then comes the call, 'Feed my sheep'. Jesus's question penetrates me during the silence. We always have a long silence, seven or eight minutes, after the reading of the Gospel for personal prayer and meditation, or simply in order to breathe, resting in God. It is a time to hear the Gospel echoing in our lives, even if no specific thoughts or insights are forthcoming. Of course your attention wanders, but you can keep coming back to the words you have just heard, and abandon yourself patiently to them once again.

Today, in this long silence, I listen: 'Let yourself be touched to the depths by the life of that man rummaging in the garbage can, by "the oui girls", by the priest in his chapel full of sculptures radiating an invisible light. You don't have to preach in public places or accomplish spectacular feats, just let your way of seeing people and situations be transformed, trusting in that which lies beyond appearances. Don't give up hope in any person or situation. Look with an eye that condemns no one. You believe that today I rise within every man or woman who suffers, in every situation of oppression that you encounter. It is up to you to accompany me in my pilgrimage as the Crucified Lord, going from one person to the next, trusting in my love, which alone is capable of bringing about the salvation of the world.'

3

People Called to Justice

COPS in San Antonio

The portly policeman in downtown San Antonio couldn't believe his ears when I asked him for the address of COPS. Finally, after having noticed that I was not going to give up, he whispered that it was definitely dangerous to walk over there. He gave me, moreover, the impression that I had to justify why I wanted to go to that part of town. 'The Amtrak station?', he asked finally, giving me a first indication of the kind of neighbourhood in which COPS is located.

To prevent him from walking away in anger, I started to explain in the midst of the traffic that COPS stands for 'Community Organized for Public Service' and that this community organization, inspired by the theories of a certain Alinsky in Chicago, had been started in San Antonio in the first part of the seventies with Ernest Cortez from St Cecilia parish, who had had that vision of awakening Mexican Americans on the West Side and of fighting for their rights as citizens against the City Council, the Good Government League, the real-estate developers, the businessmen from here to Loop 410. I told him that this process of awareness and action was considered by everybody extremely successful, last but not least by COPS itself that knows that the first rule of power tactics is to let the enemy think you have power, that COPS is a coalition of churches and had led to a revitalization of the parish life, that they had founded in the meantime a similar organization on the North Side, the Metropolitan Congregational Alliance, were planning one on the East Side and in the Valley, that a Councilman at City Hall had just told me that COPS had completely renewed the political scene of San Antonio and

57

that I wanted to make my appointment on time.

COPS has no sign on the door of its central office, which may not be unrelated to their knowing who their enemies are, an insight that must imperatively be acquired by whoever wants to join the COPS' ranks. The woman who receives me – COPS is primarily run by women and almost all the presidents up to now have been Mexican American women – is Anglo, first surprise, and a Sister of Divine Providence, second surprise. She is the metropolitan supervisor for COPS, MCA and the future East Side COPS, and has to co-ordinate strategies and to make sure that the three organizations are developing in concert with one another as well as with all the other community organizations in Texas inspired by the Industrial Areas Foundation, their consultant agency based in Huntington, New York.

I decide to start the conversation with the question of why COPS avoids undertaking actions against Kelly Air Force Base and the military installations which are some of the main sources of San Antonio's economy. My hope is that through this particular bias the originality of the COPS organization can become clearer to me. It leads us into a discussion during which the Sister, constantly friendly and later on even confidential, sometimes bangs the table with passion, especially when a prophetic vision is at stake, in order to underline her point.

She tells me that COPS is speaking out against the South Texas nuclear project which is the power plant that is built, though not in terms of anti-nuclear preoccupations but in terms of the 'crushing' economy. COPS is not a 'liberal' organization. The Mexican American people they work with tend to be more conservative than liberal. The power people, the old Anglo power structure deliberately kept San Antonio a cheap labour town. They wanted only tourist industries and nothing else that could compete on the labour market. That way they could have plenty of maids and busboys and dishwashers and pay them very low wages. The only other institution in San Antonio that offered the

Mexican Americans any sizable employment were the military bases. A lot of Mexican Americans who went through very poor schools and whose prospect for jobs were uniquely manual labour jobs with very low wages, but who were smart people, went into the military base jobs. The first president of the COPS organization (to be president is a full-time job, but not a paid one; only two staff members, organizers, are paid) who is 'one of the smartest men' the Sister has ever met, was told as a youth that he was not 'college material'. At the technical school he skipped grades, because he was so good. But the only job opening with a future and a salary for a man like him was Kelly Air Force Base. 'Those things have been good for them, they haven't been bad, they may be based on the military thing, but you are not going to cut their own throats and speak out.' The Sister is indignant against liberals who speak out on issues that will in no way affect themselves.

What does 'conservative' mean in the COPS' thinking? COPS people are interested in preserving institutions that they value, their family, their neighbourhood, their parishes (the three pillars of the IAF community organization ideology of the Southwest). A lot of people have an image of COPS – she means the Mexican-Americans – as if they were all welfare people, but they are good hard-working people. Mexican-Americans on the West Side would rather work than go on welfare. The focus is: what affects your family? What is it in the environment that makes it really hard to raise your family?

The education issue is now at the forefront of the COPS' actions. COPS had attempted to address this issue some years ago, without much result. They lost that battle, although generally their strategy is to take on only issues, however limited, that can be won; victories build up power and the image your opponents have of your power. They have come back with this same issue now, because COPS is in a better power position. The basic structural problem concerning education in San Antonio is the fact that they don't have one school district that would service the whole city. The reason is that, when San Antonio started growing, wealthy people began building suburbs, moving in all directions. The first suburb was Alamo Heights. The people there made their own school district. Others moved to Edgewood, at one time Anglo but now mostly Mexican-American with a few blacks. Then the Anglos moved to the South Side, and when the Mexicans moved in, they moved out further and further. Then they started North East and North West. The result is that there are now fifteen independent school districts. What finances the school is the property tax, with the result that each district finds resources within its own area, instead of having one school district for the whole city with a common pot.

The Edgewood school district, which covers the West Side, is the second poorest in San Antonio. There are mainly small homes, often dilapidated, no industries, no major businesses, although through COPS efforts an electric company office, a huge HEB, a movie theatre and small businesses settled in Edgewood recently. So they don't have anything to tax. In Alamo Heights, a very wealthy bedroom community on the North Side, people are able to bring in around 1100 dollars per pupil, while Edgewood can only afford 100 dollars. At the same time they pay the highest property taxes, because there are no industries to tax. 'This is a miserable inequity. The South, the West and the East Side are like third world countries compared with the North Side.' COPS is therefore trying to obtain legislation that would make a difference and consolidate financially the school systems of the poor areas. 'If they mix their money, the political entities can remain intact as well as the schoolboards. They should divide the money equally per pupil and not have Alamo Heights sitting over here with all that money. That's going to just turn the city inside out.'

This is what COPS has been trying to do over the past nine years, saying in effect: there will be no growth on the North Side unless the West Side gets its growth as well. The

Sister: 'We are not going to be the dumping ground for your water, we are not going to be the dumping ground for your sewage, we are not going to be the last people who get everything, we are not going to take the leftovers. We will be taking the thing with our own hands and you are going to deal with us.' The hope is that when MCA and the East Side COPS really get off the ground, COPS' political case on this issue will be even stronger. Basically the question they ask is: why do you force our kids to go to poor schools? Why do we have poorly paid jobs? Why don't we get an answer to those questions? 'If the whole city can't answer half the city's questions, then they have no place to go but to give in.'

Other upcoming issues are related to the question of how more relationships could come about within the neighbourhoods themselves, how people could relate to one another, how they could watch out for one another. COPS' success is of course very much linked with the constant mobilization of their people, who need to see improvements in their immediate area. Actions on the political scene are not enough; they have to be accompanied by actors rather than spectators, if COPS wants to remain the expression of the people themselves. For the Sister, 'COPS is good mental health'. It energizes the people, gives them a purpose, shows them how to build up an action and change things. It also keeps them out of apathy. After an action is completed (and 'the war won') people have a tendency to withdraw again, to become passive. She thinks this tendency to resignation, to death, ultimately has something to do with 'original sin'. People constantly have to be 'agitated' to be in relationship with others, because only then they will not be afraid of one another.

I speak about my observation of the complete separation between white Anglo Protestants on the North Side and Mexican American Catholics. People on the North Side told me that they would never go into the West Side with all those murders and killings; even if they would go, they wouldn't know what to say. Does she know any examples of people or small groups who have crossed those lines? The answer is very clear. The breakthrough will not happen with small groups, only with efforts like COPS and the MCA (in which Protestant congregations are involved). In these organizations North Side and West and South Side – and later the East Side – can get together around the table and 'negotiate' where their interests are. To go to the West Side as an individual wouldn't make sense. People would ask: who is this strange person? The problem for the people on the North Side is that they are of course willing to love their neighbour, but they don't know how, they have never had the context in which this love can express itself. COPS and the MCA offer the opportunity 'to operate as communal people', which is much more effective than individual charity. So the ideal would be to organize all the churches in San Antonio and to reflect together about what we as Christians can do? The Sister refers to the Archbishop's pastoral letter where he asks *all* parishes in the archdiocese, urban and rural, to go through the parish development process worked out by COPS and the IAF. The process consists of three steps. First, a reflection about the question of what it means to be the church, so that people understand their mission and ministry. Secondly, relationship-building within and between the churches by constantly sending the people out in order to know what people's concerns and needs are and bringing them back and reflecting with them about actions that should be undertaken. Thirdly, action for justice, significant action by the parish as a group that is decided to change their situation.

I remember attending meetings and seeing women, housewives with a sixth-grade education, standing up and making very articulate pronouncements. What must that have meant for their children to see their mother or father stand up and say in front of two hundred people 'I think ...'. Having made possible that sense of dignity and self-affirmation is in itself a tremendous accomplishment of the

COPS movement, and should cause some reflection among people who are scandalized about the rowdy methods of COPS. In spite of this, however, many parishes don't take part in it. Even for Catholic parishes it is voluntary to belong to COPS. I see that this is a delicate question for the Sister. She says that action for justice is not something we should be able to choose or not, because it is the heart of the Gospel. 'If everybody would understand the mandate, they would be in COPS.' Those who criticize the 'rude' COPS style have not measured the suffering of the people, their void in not knowing any more what is right and what is wrong, the power tactics of the wealthy, the 'original sin' of resignation, the disintegration of society and the devastating values of a TV-centred existence in which the Church is more and more unable to be a guide and a beacon.

The question regarding anti-nuclear action is still bothering her, I notice. She says that one can organize people only if the problem can be related to their experiences, if it can be broken down to that level. It's easy, I say, to break down the nuclear issue. Could the COPS method – networking, finding what people are interested in and capitalizing on that – be used for instance regarding the Central American issue? Recently, a videotape about Salvadoran refugees in Honduras was shown at Christ the King and the people from the parish felt concerned, firstly because the refugees could have been from any *barrio* in San Antonio, secondly because of the poverty situation so similar to theirs. But she thinks that neighbourhood problems are more pressing. There are people who can't afford to be concerned about those world issues. They influence the whole economy, I say. The Sister: 'I'm not worried about feeding five kids, I'm not worried about losing my job, I can afford to be worried about the world. But our people don't have the leisure for worldwide issues.' I give some examples of communities, like the Sojourners in Washington, DC, where neighbourhood concerns and world issues are constantly related and linked with one another. The Sister,

63

visibly more angry now, says that she can't get someone who thinks worldwide to become concerned about problems on the West Side. 'They operate out of their own head. We could go to those people and say, COPS is going to do a real tough action on education, and we are going to get those politicians inside out, we must have our schools different.' But the reaction would be that such a problem appears to be insignificant in comparison with the Third World and nuclear issues.

For the Sister, organizing is the most hopeful, energetic experience she has ever known. But the organizer has to have faith; without faith there is no way to come across. A few people are enough to unlock energy among many. She refers to parishes on the South Side where she tries to stimulate parish development through training-sessions. She does not always find faith on the South Side. But for her, part of the organizing is never to give up on people. Agitating people out of their apathy does not mean to force them, but to stir them up, to free energy. She finds a lot of hope in lay people. 'The face of the earth can be renewed with lay people.' Priests by and large are very depressed, have lost faith, are very difficult to deal with. 'One of my main jobs is simply to try to energize the life of priests.'

The word 'success' comes back many times in this conversation. COPS has built up an image of being successful. 'You build power and if you are smart enough about it you can expand power. The combination of the right climate and some very smart strategy put COPS in the arena of action and made other groups and institutions in San Antonio deal with COPS.' That is what power is, to make people deal with you. Everything came together for COPS at the right moment, especially by winning the fight in 1977 for the redistricting of the city, which made it possible to elect the councilmen by districts rather than at large so that Mexican Americans could be represented. One of the elements of their success was the late Archbishop Furey's decision to support COPS.

64

COPS will not go away; it is here to stay for a long, long time. Ernest Cortez has left for Houston, the other organizers don't continue their work in one place for more than two years after having awakened others for leadership, but in the meantime COPS has implanted itself on the metropolitan scene. Impressed herself, the Sister says: 'There will probably never be any other organization in the United States so incredibly powerful as COPS'.

She wants to explain again the term 'conservative' after I have remarked that COPS works out of the assumption that the Church is still viable, that there are still people in the Church. Not only does COPS work on that assumption, but it wants to rebuild those institutions; it takes what would be a dying, non-viable institution and makes it viable, preserves, conserves the institution by breathing new life into that institution. 'The institution of the Church happens to be the only one left that really can be useful to families.' For COPS the function of the Church, as part of her mission to renew the earth, is to play a role in the public arena. The Church ought to use its power in order to be more useful to their families. But the Church needs strategy. Today people try to find out what their values are, what is right and wrong, from the TV set. The only authority they relate to is television. 'The Church ought to be what TV is for the people': a place where they find significant relationships, where the issues of the world are discussed, where hurts and pains are shared, where actions for justice are started. In the past 'the unions played that role, the neighbourhood, the ward system in Chicago, my father looked at the union, the union at the Democratic Party, but if all those institutions people trusted are going bankrupt, people don't know any more what is right and what is wrong'. In this void the Church should act. 'The nuclear thing has to be raised, but in the meantime society is disintegrating, we don't know what is right and what is wrong.' That is where she sees her task, at the bottom of society, building up relationships, 'reweaving the whole fabric of society, brick by brick'. She sometimes fears that she is not working fast enough; putting brick after brick after brick is painstaking. But if it is not done, she says, people might one day even welcome a nuclear disaster.

A Black Christ painted by a Mexican priest

In the big rectory close to Holy Family in Chicago, one room is used as a chapel. One evening I attend Mass in that room with the priests and the sisters who work in the area. One of them has a home Bible programme and goes every day to the public housing area for a Bible study with families; she meets with a hundred to a hundred and twenty people once a week, many of them belonging to non-Catholic churches. The Catholic sister has become part of the life of those black families. We are facing one another, sitting in homely armchairs but a sidelong glance allows me to catch a glimpse of a painting obviously depicting a black Christ. It stands on the chimney beyond the altar. One eye expresses a deep suffering, the other one incredible anger. There is something piercing in the look of this black Christ, a blend of aggressiveness and yielding sweetness. It was painted by one of the priests, a Mexican, for 'Mad Dog', a leader in the black power movement in the sixties.

During his theology studies the young Mexican spent almost every day in the neighbourhood, walking in the streets, meeting people, making friends, fascinated by what was going on. The black power movement was a separatist movement that wanted no contact with the white community. But the Mexican found himself extremely well accepted. Being Mexican was a plus and it was easy for him to come close to the people. One day he had a conversation lasting several hours with 'Mad Dog', the leader of the black power group in the area. For him, Christ was nothing but a brainwash that came from the white man. The seminarian tried to explain, but whatever he tried he could not convince him. Back in his room he thought about the fact that he had never seen a picture of a black Christ that would appeal,

66

especially in those days of tremendous antagonism. So he decided to draw a black Christ.

Earlier this young Mexican had discovered the vocation of becoming an artist. As a child he had painted, starting with cartoons. Later, as a teenager, he had tried to copy famous pictures. More and more he felt attracted to draw out of his own inspiration, without copying or reproducing existing art, and he found in it a certain fulfilment. But now he worked on Christ. When he had finished it he went to sleep, but every hour he got up again and looked at it. The next day he went to see 'Mad Dog' and told him that he wanted to show him something, a picture of Christ. 'Mad Dog' looked at it and looked at it, he kept looking at it for a long time and said finally: 'Him I can talk to'. And because he was also a reporter he published it in the local newspaper. The seminarian exulted, went to the chapel and fell on his knees thanking God for using him an an instrument for delivering his message.

Much later a priest took the picture to the Loyola University Press and although the editor had reacted reluctantly at first, he wanted to see it. After having looked at it a long time, he showed it to one of the employees, an Italian lady. 'Who is this picture of?' he asked. She looked and after a while showed a tremendous smile. She said: 'That is the Lord'. So the editor decided to make five thousand reproductions. They were sold in three months and had to be reprinted. They went faster and had to be reprinted again. The picture went all over the country. At a demonstration in North Carolina in wintertime, a person in the first row was holding the picture walking through the snow. The picture had an impact above all in Catholic circles, although the Mexican priest has received orders for murals from Baptist churches on the South Side as well as from Lexington, Kentucky. A black Christ is definitely a symbol of social consciousness in religion. To accept the white Good Shepherd leaves things as they are. To accept the black Christ can lead to a dramatic change. Black

Catholics are accepting such an image perhaps more easily, because having joined the Catholic Church and coming from elsewhere they are more open to change. They had to adapt themselves to a new religion and having done that they are more inclined to see Jesus in a different way. The Catholic Church has certainly attempted to enable and to encourage social change. At least a theology exists that supports social justice as well as the integration of people's own traditions.

A very realistic image of Christ hurts somehow, whether it represents a white, a brown or a black person. At least we can listen to the message that comes from it. And is that message not that Christ, Image of the Invisible, the living One who precedes the pilgrimage of all humanity, shares in the agony of those who are oppressed and persecuted?

Social justice in New Orleans: the main organizing clusters

After having spent the whole day at the Archdiocesan offices, it is a pleasure to toss about in the streetcar along prestigious St Charles Avenue, with its splendid antebellum villas, the shadowy parks in which the evening sun shines around silhouettes of students who jog, jostle and jump around after a day in classrooms. Oleanders stand along the way and their leaves welcome the quaint passage of the last of the city's streetcars that has gained as much notoriety as the cable cars on Nob Hill in San Francisco. I'm looking for the Institute of Human Relations at Loyola University. The reason is the delicate question of social justice leadership in the city. In a traditionally Catholic city the influence of the Church could be powerfully wielded towards all the issues that have to do with a change in unjust structures. All the initiatives that are taken in this field, however, seem to remain timid because of lack of support by the leadership in the diocese. The Archdiocese, so strong in social services, is weak in criticizing unjust structures and in changing them. The social apostolate is privately financed by an annual appeal and breakfasts where the people come with their chequebooks ready; it does not depend on government assistance. National cutbacks will not affect the social ministry the Archdiocese has chosen. On the other hand, some people say that this dependence on private gifts limits the freedom to act prophetically in causes that play a role at the Capitol in Baton Rouge. Furthermore, the Archbishop has made it perfectly clear that he himself is opposed to the nuclear freeze, is opposed to union organizing and favours capital punishment. How should priests, religious and lay people who have a different vision act, if they feel the lack of support of the whole church and see themselves going against the directional signals that come from Walmsley Avenue? It certainly restrains a certain number of people from going ahead with actions they perceive as a priority. For this reason it is not surprising that leadership for social justice issues comes from the university milieu and in particular from Jesuits, who being a religious order are somehow outside of the immediate jurisdiction of the Archdiocese, while being profoundly implanted in the New Orleans society.

The Institute of Human Relations, led by a young Jesuit, functions like a consultant agency, developing relationships between people working on different issues, analysing them, showing the interconnection of all the issues, participating with groups in planning and management assistance, even getting grants for those groups. It is not only an intellectual institute, as one would suspect from its location on the Loyola campus' grounds; it is an activist place. Today a meeting is taking place with twenty-five mostly Catholic church people and TEAM people. TEAM is the Teamsters, Engineers, ACORN movement, an effort by three labour unions to come together to organize the hotel and hospital workers in the city. Hotel workers, mostly black and Vietnamese, are laid off in the slow summer season, get minimum wages while not working all year round. The United Labour Union Local 100 is affiliated with ACORN, which is in charge of the organizing. The Teamsters bring in most of the money; the Engineers, in addition to some money, contribute staff people. The aim of the meeting today is to get the churches involved. The institute has been asked to make the contacts and to get the ball rolling for a new co-operation between unions and churches that would allow a neighbourhood approach to union organizing. Here in New Orleans they think this is the first structural possibility the churches will have had to take part in an effort for economic justice in the city. If they get it off the ground, they think they will have set an important precedent for other poverty programmes in the city. It is conceived as a three-year campaign, led by fifteen organizers, some of them highly trained. Before asking the big hotels for recognition, they need to build up a lot of strength in the city. First of all they will have to get the Vietnamese themselves on board in order to prevent the hotel managers from using them to scare the blacks and by threatening that if blacks join the union Vietnamese only will be hired. But to get bases in the city and support, the churches' involvement is necessary. Building up relationships with a lot of churches will take time. The TEAM churches will be invited to make their facilities available, to preach about the rights of the workers and have a contact person in the parish who co-ordinates visits and meetings with hotel and hospital workers living in the surrounding area. This organizing cluster is new and could open many other avenues for action in favour of the working poor.

The biggest problem in New Orleans is poverty, according to the analysts at the institute. New Orleans is the lowest of the nation's largest cities in *pro capita* income. This does not mean that they have the highest unemployment rate – they don't – but the highest underemployment. They have the largest proportion of people who work full-time and don't make a living wage, especially in the tourist industry and the health-care centres. There are not enough jobs or manufacturing industries in the city. The mayor is addressing this question by developing a whole section out in New Orleans East for industry. A high tech factory from California is located there and negotiations are underway for getting Renault to start manufacturing buses. In the meeting somebody speaks at length about a brand-new building that is ready to give vocational training – in the perspective of fifteen hundred job openings – but that can't be used because the State government is unable to give the money for staff, equipment, computers and teachers. Since the downward trend of the oil industry the State government has lost a lot of oil taxes and seems to be going bankrupt. In addition the laws ensure that wealth remains concentrated in the hands of a minority.

The Churches haven't struck the analysts as having a history of sensitivity to social justice problems. However, at the present time a lot of good people seem to be starting to question the social order. The contemporary concern about nuclear war is a good point of entry for many church people in New Orleans because they are beginning to realize that there is a relationship between military spending and the problems of the poor, because of the tremendous effect it has on interest rates, unemployment and public benefits for people without means. They also see a more grassroots leadership emerging that is very competent. One group that is acting against a nuclear power plant, for instance, will be working together with another one that is forcing the State to stop cutting people off from welfare. Connections are being made. If only the Churches would involve themselves in a re-education of the clergy. . . . They say that the clergy still have a traditional view of things that keeps them from getting involved. They don't read up on the issues. Clergy and laity are still afraid of the connection between faith and social justice. There is a need for innovative ways of thinking on spirituality that would integrate prayer and contemporary needs.

Black churches are strong supporters of the Louisiana Survival Coalition, a state-wide organizing and lobbying

71

group. This black initiative was born some years ago at a big meeting with a thousand people in Baton Rouge at the Catholic Life Centre. People came from all over the State. They have strong organizers and build on their first successes. When the State passed its ten-year reapportioning plan changing the boundaries of the districts for the legislature in function of the population shifts as reflected by the new census figures, it was presented in a way that would have reduced the number of black seats. The Survival Coalition went to court, forced them to stop and to do it over again. When the State cut eight hundred families off from welfare because of a new 'monthly reporting form', Survival organized an action in order to limit as much as possible the damage to the public assistance programme for the poor. They also have task forces that work on issues like utility rights. Slowly they are spreading their influence, focusing on Baton Rouge where fifty people showing up with a bus still impress the legislature, while in Washington the same thing happens every day and therefore doesn't have the same direct influence any more.

The third organizing cluster the Human Institute values very much is the Louisiana Coalition on Jails and Prisons, which seems to be one of the best groups advocating changes in the criminal justice system. They have a strong infrastructure, a very competent staff and have been successful in getting some of the standards changed as well as getting the ball rolling concerning certain federal court suits. Religious leaders have organized, ecumenically, a related action against the death penalty. It is interesting to hear that the young Jesuit who presides over the Institute is the chairman of this ecumenical group, is at the heart of the TEAM initiative and sits in on the steering committee of the Survival Coalition. Coalition for Action, a community organization, has not been able to keep a solid structure and healthy financing. They had a lot to do with housing but more in relationship with middle-class people than with the poor. The good organizers have left and the organization is in deep trouble.

The hope is that out of these initiatives other actions will flow, in particular in the field of education. If those who work on public government action or the working poor or the prisons and jails or education could keep in touch with one another, some broadly based organization could start that would speak out with a lot of authority. The analysts, because of this hope, say that New Orleans could be in worse shape.

A home for runaways in the Bay Area

A home for homeless teens is no sinecure. During the first week of November things seemed peaceful, however. One was in school – she has been to twenty schools in sixteen years – another working full time. An ex-resident stopped by to say hello, casually mentioning that she had been bleeding for a month. An hour later she was at Kaiser Hospital for an emergency operation. Another ex-resident dropped by on the same evening and went to the hospital to visit the first one. While visiting, the police arrived and put him in jail. The volunteers at the house gathered and phoned doctors, lawyers and friends to aid the teens. At 11pm the Burlingame police department called to say that another ex-resident had been beaten and robbed. They picked him up at 2am at Mills Hospital.

The house looks like so many other American wooden villa-style homes: the paint is coming off, the garden is a wilderness, a few trucks loaded with boxes stand around. Somebody with a broad smile, sentimental and tough at the same time, who must have some charming power over people, introduces me to the teens draped across couches and looking at TV. He started this house six years ago and is working on the building of another home for infants and children up to ten years of age, battered babies and children caught in violent divorce disputes. His only contact with the Catholic Worker prior to starting this house was an experience in a Catholic Worker house in San Jose, a place for street alcoholics, a shelter for twenty people and a feeding place for one hundred and twenty others. He had read about the Catholic Worker and 'just stumbled into it'. The man has been a priest for ten years. The first three he worked in a parish in Pacifica but 'raising money and building churches was really not what I was about'. He wanted to do something closer to the people. It took him four years of 'dabbling', trying this, trying that, to figure out what to do. For instance he spent time community organizing in Alinsky's style. He noticed that the method moved large numbers of people very rapidly, but he is not tender in his criticism because he thinks the method could be used just as well to develop a Hitler Youth movement in an area. He calls it a brittle method that does very good things with good leaders who are well informed and trustworthy, but the self-interest at the heart of it can lead to perversions. He organized senior citizens to march on Sacramento and they had six thousand people in half a year, as he acknowledges now, for selfish reasons. Not that they didn't do good things but it would have been possible, he thinks, to reverse it and to get the same people to do something that is in their own interest because they hate black people. He sees in it more 'mass mob control' than education and motivation because 'people don't know why they do what they're doing'. So he decided to quit and to spend a year reading and thinking. For the first six months of that year he lied when people asked 'What are you doing?' He would make up things and make it sound important. After about six months he learned that it was all right to tell people 'I'm doing nothing, I sit in my room, I read, I write, I play with the kids on the block, I take walks'. People didn't believe him. He lived near a cemetery and walked there. Late at night, if he couldn't sleep and had enough money to buy a beer, he walked to a bar called 'The Stumble Inn', with his pen and paper. It was a bad time. 'Like water and sand it takes a while to sink in, calm things down. I'd get blown this way and that way by the winds.'

During the last year of looking he moved to a community called Belmont, not far from Redwood City. A married couple and their children moved into the same neighbourhood. Another family and their four children were there as well, all within a couple of blocks of one another. He lived with another priest and another single male electrician. They met together along with a few other people every week, praying, studying, bringing in speakers, to try to study and pray their way to action. It didn't work. After one year, the couple with the two kids went to El Salvador to work with the poor. The couple with the four kids ended up at a Catholic Worker farm. One of the women in the group went to a monastery. Another went up to San Francisco and started a kitchen for Puerto Rican women. He went to the Catholic Worker house in San Jose. He was more and more into feeding, clothing, sheltering the poor and heavily involved in resistance to nuclear weapons; he spent some time in jail.

His choice was to start this home for teenagers, and to become their family. The teens come from jail, from hospitals, from their families, from the street. The only common denominator among them is that they are people who have been under a lot of pressure and who have cracked. Some of them are into drugs or alcohol. Some are runaways, some are suicidal. None of them have families they can live with. The one whom he is asking about her temperature, telling her to take a lot of liquid, soft drinks, to go to bed or to watch TV while we are sitting in the kitchen with a glass of wine, is thirteen and has been broken many times; 'we are the best thing that ever happened to her'.

Three men live in the house as volunteers. Two women work with them; it was too difficult for them to live in the house with the rough teenagers and with the men who set a workaholic tone. When teenagers come to the house, they pay nothing. If they work they have to give their cheques that are put in a trustee account for them. They get it back when they leave. They either have to go to work full-time, go to school full-time or do fifty-fifty but they have to be busy all day, every day. If they want the house to be a motel or a boarding house, they have to leave. They stay as long as they need to, being part of the other's lives and vice versa. I meet one girl who has been there about seven months; she has a good job and over a thousand dollars in the bank. She could move out on her own but she is still not quite ready. Others are ready after a month or two.

Elsewhere one will find homes and institutions working on behalf of the young, but here they live together. The vulnerability of the volunteers is much greater. Every teenager has an array of problems. If there are legal problems, a lawyer has to be found. If there are medical problems, a doctor has to be found. Most of them have psychological problems. Some of them need to see a therapist. Many of them have educational problems. They may have to get them put in a special school. All of them have personal problems. They may be pregnant or have a boyfriend. They don't know about birth control. They may never have met an adult they could talk to. 'Sex, booze and money are key issues in these kids' lives and if they don't have somebody to talk to that knows what they're talking about, they will be in trouble, so we get down to the practicalities like that rather rapidly.' They have a network of volunteers who help the kids. But living with them there is of course very emotionally demanding. 'You're walking past one another in your pyjamas. You're seeing laughing and crying. You're dealing with their parents if they have them. You're dealing with the lack of parents if they don't have them. And at least once a month there is a major catastrophe.'

They take a maximum of six but they try to keep it down to four. More would turn the home into a hospital. As a Catholic Worker House they don't only want to meet the needs of the poor but also to be a model for the people around as a family. They have only a few families to whom they could send a teenager. If a family already has teenagers, they worry about their own; if they have infants, they would worry for their safety; if they are older people, they fear they will not be able to understand the kids. But they are able to find lawyers, doctors, dentists, eye specialists, or somebody who cooks meals and the food is all donated. Specific commitments for a limited length of time are possible. 'Instead of going to a plumber and asking him to take a course on baptism, we ask him as a plumber, we honour what he is good at.' They have no financial problems at all because there is no problem convincing people that what is being done in general for teenagers is not working. And the homelessness of teenagers as well as the violence done to infants in the Bay Area society is epidemic. As soon as there are some people to spend time with them, the support is awesome. They could easily have five homes like this full all the time. 'The first year that we opened this home there were four thousand teenagers in this county that went to jail. I used to be chaplain up at the jail. At least half, maybe more, would not be there if there was a place to put them.' A study was made in a neighbouring county saying that five thousand children ran away from home in one year. They go to the street, to jail, to friends.

Facing all this, do they want to expand, start an 'Under 21' like in New York? They want to keep it 'small is beautiful'. Dan Berrigan wrote them a note at the start saying: 'Remember, good things start small and get smaller'. 'Under 21' is a gigantic institution with a multi-million-dollar budget, they want to solve the problem of the young people in a megapolis like New York. Here they have taken the option not to institutionalize people's problems, to start juvenile homes that are more like jails than they are homes or day-care centres or convalescent homes. 'You just cannot take care of people's problems by hiring people to do it. It's like trying to pay a shepherd.'

They would rather invite a thousand families to give one room each for one person than build a building where they would be housed together. As the old saying puts it, there is no survival outside the church, which means outside a communion of people. 'You either become part of what some of us would call the body of Christ or a family or a friendship or whatever kind of communion or you've had it, and in our society, as the forces pull people away from one another, a lot of us have had it.'

He compares himself with Orville Wright inventing the aeroplane. People must have said: 'Even if this stupid thing flies, how are you going to move a thousand people from New York to San Francisco? We've got the covered wagon. Why not use it?' The aeroplane got off the ground and went a hundred and some feet. People say to the volunteers in this house: 'Don't waste your time because even if it works, what's your solution for the whole society?' But right now it is flying. Somebody else has to figure out how a small loving community can become a society. And if it crashes, as he thinks anything that makes sense does in this society, I'm sure Christ will be his parachute.

A Baptist ministering to seamen

It is easy to forget that Manhattan is an island. But today I meet with a Baptist minister who works at the Seamen's Church Institute on State Street, at the tip of Manhattan. Through the window I will see beyond Battery Park this passing seascape of swells, ships and sailor stories swallowed up between Manhattan, Ellis Island, Liberty Island, Governor's Island and Staten Island in the distance. For at least a century each ripple carried flotillas of hope – the greatest number arriving around 1910 – which sheltered the living and the survivors of the European shores. Holding up under the difficult trials of separation, crossing and arrival, these men and women were taking the unfathomable risk of investing in the American dream all their hopes, especially those dreamed for their children. I am not so sure that the two hundred thousand persons who daily use the Staten Island ferry, nor the half million who come to work in

Lower Manhattan, all taken up by their own future, remember each time in whose footsteps they walk; but what would their lives be today without the sacrifices of those coming from that distant horizon, men and women standing in awe of at least being here, on the threshold of a new life?

Because I took the wrong subway, I find myself walking a section of Broadway. The Trinity church carillon gently rejoices over those who take a noon break in the sun. My ears pick up a sound, a very old tune of a Christmas carol from Picardy, France. I have forgotten the words. But upon entering the church I hum along with it, so I will not forget it. As I bump into and interrupt a woman selling some object of devotion to my well-dressed neighbour, she answers my pressing question by saying she was not paying attention. An endless discussion ensues. Four of us find ourselves up in arms, mutually interrupting one another on the linguistic origin of the word 'carillon': French? Dutch? I probably gave them a slight shock as I abruptly moved away still humming the same melody for fear of forgetting it. I walk in the minister's office at the SCI. He immediately opens his hymnal to the very hymn:

'Rank on rank the host of heaven
Spreads its vanguard on the way,
As the light of light descendeth
From the realms of endless day,
That the powers of hell may vanish
As the darkness clears away.'

Having found it makes me as happy as a child. It will remain like a resounding melody in our encounter, like good news just heard which gives infinite rejoicing.

I stand in the office of a man who has known our Community since the fifties; a man filled with passion at the emergence of monastic life in Protestantism; a man at that time in touch with creative forces in Europe which were reflected at Bossey, Villigst, in the lay training academies of Germany. Being the son and grandson of Baptist ministers, he was involved in an active search for the renewal of the

Church; as a matter of fact he met with the founder of our Community back in 1955 in Cambridge, at Krister Stendahl's home. He had often heard the annual anti-Catholic sermons that preachers, often ex-priests who had jumped the wall, came to deliver in the temples of his youth. He had also read 'People's Padre', an anti-Catholic book which sold like hot cakes. Yet he was ardently searching for a new way to link deep spiritual life and social awareness as well as a commitment to go beyond the ritual Sunday hour. He then took the initiative of inviting two of our brothers to come and work with him at Packard Manse in Boston. In the early sixties, this student house was becoming a 'yeasty place', as he would say, from where initiative after initiative was launched. He told me the brothers had dropped in, unannounced, on Cardinal Cushing – in 1960 there were no contacts between Catholics and Protestants – and that the Cardinal, who was to become a great friend of the Community, had later said: 'I was going to throw these two bums out of the house!' Awkward beginnings of ecumenism. . . .

The originality of Packard Manse and its young leader was to invite pastors, priests and lay persons for prayer and a meal in a very simple spirit of welcome; the visitors were to experience an encounter with others up to now ignored, feared, crushed, rejected. The first time they shared a meal together such things were heard as: I've been preaching against you all my life ... a solidarity is born from the simple fact of doing dishes together to be ready for common prayer. . . . One can easily imagine the extraordinary effects in the daily life of the Churches as a result of these agapes in Stoughton, fifteen miles from Boston. Packard Manse was becoming an open house releasing freshness in an atmosphere of intellectual alertness, attentive to the signs of the times. Like in many other areas of the world, what was going on there was an anticipation of what was going to spread in a spectacular way, as did for example Vatican II, in a deep movement of hope. My host describes the vocation of Packard Manse at that time as the search for reconciliation among divided persons, particularly at first between Catholics and Protestants. A concrete result to come out of this was a uniting of the eleven theological seminaries of the Greater Boston Area into the Boston Theological Institute. This search for reconciliation naturally made the participants aware of other divisions besides those between confessional institutions. They were still too steeped in ideas to tackle in a practical way the divisions in Boston itself between blacks and whites, but were very much vibrating to the struggle in the South. Later on, before the Yom Kippur war in 1967, courses on relations between Jews and Christians were begun and alternately held in a synagogue and a church. In the seventies the division between the wealthy Northern hemisphere and the poor Southern hemisphere deepened their constant ecumenical endeavour.

A certain knack to catch what is in the air; a place for spontaneous meetings; an awareness for many of the new steps to be taken; nothing however linked these persons in a more definite way. And so this is how communities come and go ... but who will know how many persons were motivated or remotivated for the renewal of the life of the Churches? Packard Manse was not a new Church; there was nothing on Sunday morning. Its only goal was to stir things up, to open avenues of reflection and action without becoming itself the answer. All institutionalization was rejected, thus it was willing to disappear in order to make space for the Spirit. To be a thoroughfare in a time of grace, without wanting to hold back the Spirit, to seek out in these depths of inspiration more lasting personal commitments wherever life would lead each one – that was the goal.

Regardless of the difference of structure with Taizé, which is a monastic community based on commitments for life, the Packard Manse leader kept his eye on it. In 1980 when Brother Roger led an evening of prayer in a packed St Patrick's Cathedral, he was there. At the end of the evening, when the participants of this pilgrimage of reconciliation took the streets towards St Peter's for another time of prayer, he walked in the candlelight of the night next to Brother Roger, just to pray and to chant the ongoing repeated 'Adoramus Te, Domine'. It was enough for him, as he walked silently behind the cross, to call to mind those twenty-five years of companionship, to walk side by side in the silence of mutual attention.

Since then he has settled in New York and was ordained a minister like his father and grandfather. This installation took place at Memorial Baptist church in Harlem, where he became the only white minister in the team. In the liturgy of the ordination, black gospel music filled the air along with a Bach chorale, but on the programme he showed me I also recognized the 'Adoramus Te, Domine'.

During lunch – the menu was monkfish! – we talked about his new ministry for the men of the sea, those outcasts on dry land, arriving every day in the Brooklyn and Newark ports in twenty boats from overseas. The Institute, a private foundation with Episcopal roots, hired him as an ecumenical minister to tackle the human rights of the seafarers. In his office with soft-tempered light, without windows, he put a captain's antique desk, a model of a merchant ship, in the corner a colourful temple hanger from India, a few etchings, law books concerning the sea, and three portraits. Added to this, his fine and smiling face creates a pleasant Bostonian environment unexpected among tough and wrinkled sailors. When I arrived this morning, I found him working on a talk he will soon give at the Vatican. A portrait of Richard Henry Dana, author of the bestseller *Two years before the mast* (1840), hangs before me. Dana was the first to speak about life on the sea, in somewhat crisp details, as in the chapters on flogging or sea chanteys, as witnessed from his own experience on the brig *Pilgrim*. In no other place can one find such vivid descriptions of the crimping system of the boarding house owners who brought under total control young fellows, from New England farms, tempted by the glamour of the sea. At the turn of the century a boarding house keeper could, unpunished, get a seaman drunk and put him on a ship for a voyage of one or two years without his knowledge of the miserable living conditions on the ships. A powerful network of boarding houses broke the backs of seafarers, forcing them to surrender their personal liberty. Dana, appalled by the slavery conditions on the ships, later became an admiralty-lawyer.

The institute, located since 1834 on the waterfront of the shipping area of the nineteenth century, today works with two hundred and fifty thousand seamen. My host cares mostly for the strangers among them who come from the third world. They number one-third of the seafaring population. They are usually young in the trade and most likely will not spend the rest of their lives doing that work. But coming from unemployment situations, their hope is to make a fast dollar to buy a small farm or business. They are very different from the American seaman in his late fifties, alone and often drifting and in despair, having lost all anchors. They are also different from Moby Dick (Melville was born on this spot) or the romantic pirates of our youth, because they are often the objects of exploitation. For instance a Filipino seaman has been in a sense a prisoner on his own boat for three years, without having been paid, the reason being that the Greek captain promised him his pay at the next port. It is impossible to have any kind of recourse because the boat is registered in Panama and the owner lives in Lubeck. A number of these men are constantly in a situation of exploitation: excessive duty hours, broken contracts, subhuman living conditions. 'If one has a legal complaint, the international character of the ship becomes a problem. Despite the development in recent years of a considerable corpus of international law, there is to date no effective international law protecting individuals'. This is why my host and his colleagues, who speak twelve languages, visit each ship that docks in New York, even if they stay only a few hours. He sees this above all as a ministry of hospitality, creating an atmosphere of confidence. Whom else could a sailor from India trust with four hundred dollars to send to his family? Secondly, it is a ministry of justice. Another chaplain might offer the sailors a bus tour of the city and use it as a pretext to give a good sermon, the last frontier of missionary work. But at the SCI there is an effort to change the traditional chaplaincy into a commitment for justice. 'We seek to inform seafarers of their rights by distributing summaries of the laws that protect them. We equip chaplains, union officials, lawyers, with a bulletin, through workshops, through a network of information about those ships, ports, owners, agents that ignore basic human values, for a better job of advocacy. We are alerting shipowners, charterers, agents, unions and governments. And we work with the "human rights community", those hundreds of groups who work for human rights, to have them adopt our special cause, the forgotten international seafarer.'

Kneeling in the shrine of St Elizabeth Seton next door, I ask myself what she would recommend to us today, we who sometimes despair in the face of all the calamities that come upon the human heart in a city like New York. Would she think that there is indeed a hope that New York could become a port of welcome to the stranger, a lighthouse of freedom for the oppressed and a beacon in the stormy lives of the lowly and 'that the powers of hell may vanish, as the darkness clears away'?

4

Gospel Families

New Life Unlimited in a Chicago ghetto

You don't believe any more in the parish? You've seen it all in the Church? You don't find a spirit of sharing, communion, festival, poverty of spirit, imagination in your congregation? Please follow those visitors from Mainland China who wanted to see what people are doing in Chicago and were sent to Bethel Lutheran church west of Garfield Park. The pastor and his sister will pick you up with their truck, maybe late in the evening, in spite of the rain and a hectic day of court, awards and sweat equity. On the expressway you will feel confused, trying to listen to both speaking at the same time, about what they have been doing for fifteen years. As a refrain you will hear: 'It is a joy' but anyhow you will have understood from the very beginning that these are people for whom the Church is a burning fire, 'a spring of water that never runs dry', God's family in action, a people who rebuild what has long been in ruins, a place of total commitment. They will tell you that they arrived in 1965, three days before the riots, when the National Guard and the tanks arrived in the streets of the neighbourhood where 35,000 white people moved out of and 45,000 black people moved in, within a two-year period. They saw it as the challenge of their life to rebuild a church – that had not moved out – and to rebuild a community.

Entering into the neighbourhood, they will show you two townhouses that they are building and, on the next block, the apartments they want to rebuild through a sweat-equity co-operative, on land that they already own. A bit further, they point to a forty-unit senior citizens apartment house under construction. The very poor people from the area did some of the work on the buildings themselves. Each one has a capital account and Bethel keeps a record of it. Each month they would give them a notice saying 'you have earned this many dollars towards your part of the ownership'. Then they would meet every week with the whole group, to work out the rules by which they would be going to live together, to discuss questions of management, to set up the legal documents. Those people have never owned anything in their lives before, but now they can't blame the landlord any more . . . .

People in suburban churches are invited to share in the investment. If ten or twenty people invest one or two thousand dollars each, it helps Bethel to buy a building. Bethel will manage it and make sure that, in five years, the people living in the building will own it. During those five years the suburban people get some tax deduction, enabling Bethel to create decent places for people to live, for low prices.

Here is the Bethel New Life Centre, the headquarters for the community programme. Here they will be talking with you, amid a computer, photograph albums, records of gospel music sung by Mrs 'B' and an industrial co-operative (Stitches Unlimited making quilted nylon jackets, pile-lined quilt boots and disposable non-wovens) in the basement. The building was built in the 1890s, and used by the YMCA. Later it became a factory for fifty years. The signs say: Supreme Industrial Products Company. Bethel bought the building when the man who owned it retired. The pastor, his sister and the whole church have taken four blocks around the church and have set that as their target area for the coming years. When people drive through, they will see that something is going on in this very depressed area.

A new chapter is just beginning. Bethel has asked for affiliation with 'Habitat for Humanity', based in Americus, Georgia, in order to become the Chicago chapter of this effort. All the people in Chicago who have ever given money to 'Habitat' will be approached by Bethel. They want to start 'Habitat' and focus it on their community. That will ensure that the very, very poor will also be included. Bethel's model is: development without displacement. For the townhouses, for instance, people have to have some income, no matter how little, to be able to buy into that kind of housing. They have to pay two thousand dollars (at 6¾ per cent interest). This is still too expensive for some of the other families .... Therefore Bethel has to do some 'Habitat', with no interest and no profit, so that they can make sure there is really a mixture of people in the area and that they are not moving anybody out but provide housing for those who have nothing. The process developed by 'Habitat' is to assure that the people who get the house build both their own and the next house. Of course they have to be helped all the way along.

Today the court gave them a building. It is empty, and the structure of this three apartment house is sound. Bethel would like to make their first 'Habitat' out of it. They estimate that it will cost 25,000 dollars per apartment. If you spread that amount over twenty years and make a mortgage with no interest, it only comes out to 103 dollars per month. People can afford that. Then they get the equity for working on it. They are building up capital. The situation is similar to the townhouses for which Bethel had to raise money in order to bring the price down. Unless somebody lives in the place for five years, Bethel would buy the house back at a reduced price. Then you don't have somebody who lives there just one year and moves out, getting a lot of money. The idea is to provide housing, not to manipulate money. In New York the city is not sure any more if it will continue to sell apartments for two hundred and fifty dollars to the co-ops, because there are some examples of people who resell them for $20,000. That is why Bethel's sweat-equity co-operative is also what they call a limited sweat-equity co-operative. They only get a six per cent increase on the 350 dollars they put down in cash to own the building, plus six hundred hours of work. When they sell five years later, they will get the 350 dollars plus six per cent over five years back. This ensures that in five years, another poor person will still be able to afford it. That is why it is called a limited equity. The value stays with the building, with the whole group of people and not just the individual. 'Habitat' will help to raise the money for the first house, but it is basically Bethel's responsibility. And even with that, they still have to raise money, because paying 100 dollars a month back does not build many other houses. The costs are going up every year, and there is no interest.

All of the initiatives that Bethel has taken are based on the fundamental value of sharing between Christians, between people living in welfare conditions. The primary thing for Bethel is that God's people here are helping each other out, being the Good Samaritan in the community. It is self-help, community development – through the Church. At the same time a very strong local church has developed, almost self-supporting, although the members are poor people. On Sunday morning the church is full. Bethel is the people's thing. A lot of the suburban churches want to give clothing but they don't accept it. They don't hand out food. Poor people have something to give themselves. For instance, a Namibian paster recently came and told about the South African army having bombed and burned their printing press, the people at Bethel gave 265 dollars that Sunday. Offerings for world hunger bring 300 dollars in one month, which is even more than in many suburban churches. The key thing is that even if they don't have money, they feel God has blessed them and therefore they want to share. Bethel doesn't want to be dependent on food or clothing from a suburban church. The emphasis is on self-help, but then they ask for investment partnership. People in the parish who *are* employed are bus drivers, factory workers, labouring people. But four people give sixty dollars a week or more. Twenty families give between forty and sixty dollars. It is their commitment. The church is the most important thing in their life, the work of the church and the hope that that brings to life, a work that is something of value to them but also to the community, to the children, to the future.

There is a good spirit. Sunday morning, they say, gives them the gasoline that keeps them going all week. Bethel church is a church of celebration. They laugh, pray, cry together. The noisy celebration, two hours long, is not typically Lutheran although they sing the liturgy, and the people love it. With a smile the neighbourhood calls it the Lutheran Baptist church. They have six choirs, and three sing every Sunday, with soloists, organ and gospel music.

Most community organizations on the Westside don't run programmes but deal with issues. Bethel has organized 'Concerned Citizens of West Garfield' as a free-standing group which is not incorporated and can therefore support political candidates. It is like an arm of Bethel, colleagues but existing independently. They fight the slumlords, while Bethel is trying to convince the area's absentee landlords to hire it to manage their buildings, which would have more impact on the neighbourhood than the relatively few houses or buildings they could build or renovate.

So Bethel has a very broad scope, a church, a Christian school, a day-care centre, a community organization, a housing organization, a medical centre soon. That is the reason why they changed their name from Bethel Housing to 'Bethel New Life', because their work includes now all those things plus the wholistic centre and the economic development through Stitches Unlimited, and all those things are new life. There are three corporations involved. If one section should fail, it would not hurt the other two: one is the church incorporated which owns the two subsidiary corporations, one is Bethel Educational Services and the other is called New Life which runs the community programmes.

Writing about Bethel, a reporter spoke of a 'loaves-fishes approach'. You put many things together and they multiply. It is the same process as in the Lord's miracle. Jesus said, feed the people. They had only those few loaves and fishes. They didn't have enough. They didn't sit around complaining, they did the feeding. And Jesus *made* that enough. That is what Bethel has experienced. They never had money for anything they have started. They just start and do it, knocking on doors and putting things together and somehow it works.

Here you find Lutheran pietism at its best. The place reminds me of the towns created by the Hernhuters: a profound rootedness in the Bible, a deep spiritual life and that capacity of creating a place of hope, one step after the other, trusting God throughout the unknown, entering into all the consequences of their commitment, including the political impact. The pastor, the sister and the whole team are very clear. They say that the 'trickle down approach' does not work. They have to deal with both the cutbacks on the resources from federal programmes and the increase in individual needs because of high unemployment, increased costs and cutbacks of funds. In an era 'when government is abdicating responsibility for the poor' they try to create new partnerships with the business sector, to call people to share and to choose 'between bread and bombs in politics'.

There is a curfew in the neighbourhood after 10.30pm in order to prevent crime. So if you are lucky, they will drive you home. Will the pastor tell you that both his grandparents came as Swedish immigrants to Minnesota? His father was a minister in Washington DC and had one of the first integrated churches. The son, after his seminary in Minnesota, at the Swedish Theological Institute in Jerusalem and in Rock Island, Illinois, wanted to work in a city. But at that time they assigned you, there was no choice. And the bishop sent him out to start a new church in ... Country Club Hills, Illinois, a brand new suburb where he remained four years building up a congregation of four hundred members in the middle of the cornfields. When the building of the first unit was under way, his bishop called him up saying: didn't you want to serve in the city? And there he went to Chicago, to Bethel. 'This is my place.' After having wrestled, this was exactly what he had wanted all along, 'such a joy'. His brother lives in Seattle, has three children of his own and has adopted seven others, four blacks, two Korean and one American-Indian. This brother is very much involved in protesting against the Nuclear Trident submarine. He was put in jail several times. Last year their mother joined him. They were both in the Bay Area on a small boat when the Trident came in. 'We have not been able to stop Auschwitz. We have got to try to stop this insanity.' Their mother is almost eighty years old. Both were arrested, handcuffed and kept in detention for eight hours before being released. The trial was cancelled due to the fact that all charges were dropped. Their mother was the 1973 American Mother of the year. She is from a family of federal judges, United States Congressmen and pastors. She has written devotional books, one is called 'God's song in my heart'. Their children are extraordinarily prepared to live among the poor. They say that for them it is 'the happiest place to be'. The mother and the daughter travel every year to our European meetings, in London, Paris, Rome refreshing themselves in the prayer with the thousands of young people who take part in them.

Would you still say there is no hope in the Church?

A couple of hopeful Presbyterians in San Francisco
Is there hope for the Church in this city? Where do you see signs of hope or promising initiatives that open a road into the future? When I ask these questions, people in general enumerate first the reasons why they feel rather desperate with regard to the Church; only slowly does there emerge during the conversation the willingness to discover all that is already new, even if it is still hidden. But sitting in the small office of the San Francisco Young Adult Network on Market Street in Tenderloin, I'm in the presence of people who give me the impression of constantly re-imagining the

Church. The couple is Presbyterian. There is a Lutheran intern, a United Methodist minister and me. We bring our low seats closer to one another and share.

The problem they all feel very strongly is that the churches, especially the Protestant ones, in San Francisco, by and large are dying or are already dead, although they have not yet learned to admit it. Plus, when a church still has members and money a kind of panic induces them to a spirit of competition instead of co-operating in order to keep their own institution going. The only large, fast growing church in San Francisco is the Voice of Pentecost. An old movie theatre on Ocean Avenue houses them. They fill it night after night, showing movies for free. Big gospel choirs fill the air. Driving along I read on the marquee in bold characters 'Prophecy Hotline' plus a phone number with the assuring promise 'A new prophecy every day'. One person did it all, a seemingly unattractive woman in her sixties. The mainline Protestant denominations neither have the emotionality Pentecostals have nor the richness of liturgy or the spiritual life the Catholics or Orthodox have nor a sufficiently strong political commitment to attract people searching for justice when even timid statements chase away the bulk of the silent majority. Are there ways of reinvigorating the traditional churches?

In several parishes in San Francisco I have come across a community organizing effort that in order to build up a grass-roots power structure has involved churches and synagogues as well as labour unions. They are working with the congregations that want to come together and deal with some issues of the city. Most of the parishes that have affiliated are Catholic. Non-Catholic communities include two Methodist, one Lutheran, one UCC, one Episcopal, one Church of God in Christ and the Lutheran Latino Ministries. The San Francisco Organizing Project is still in its beginning but it already generates a lot of excitement, ecumenical coalescing, interviewing processes in congregations about their major concerns, relationships between minorities and whites, unions and churches, and the hope that through the structuring coalition of the two largest constituency organizations in the city some cohesiveness may arise that stems out of shared values, purposes and belief systems. The President of the Department Store Employees Union, local 1100 said at a meeting: 'In Shakespeare's *Coriolanus* we find the following question being asked, "What is the city but the people?" And the answer came back, "Yes, the people are the city". The SFOP sprung from the need to approach the problems of the "people" in San Francisco with the goal of bringing various segments of society together, in a bridge-building social consciousness programme.' The objective is to develop a power structure that helps its members make the changes they want to see happen in San Francisco. This can only come about if the inner life of the participating groups is strengthened. And the self-interest of parishes comes in here. In a multicultural parish like St Elizabeth this brings four hundred people together in a parish convention in order to define their major concerns: meeting the needs of the elderly, resolving the issue of a Junior High School property, installing a new pipe organ, bringing middle-aged people together for friendship and formation of a crime committee. The concerns may seem removed from burning overall issues in the city; the organizers have patience. Old St Mary's church was able to make a stand concerning the rent stabilization law in Chinatown. At St John the Evangelist it has strengthened their sense of community and 'we begin and end meetings on time, for the most part, and the problem of co-ordinating the coffee hour which has hung like an albatross round the necks of many a hostess has been solved'. One day all these communities will be linked in a city-wide organization that would be multi-ethnic, cross-cultural, inter-religious and speak out about quality education, decent and affordable housing, safe neighbourhoods, civil and equal rights, health care, employment opportunities, racial-cultural-generational tensions in favour of

93

the unrepresented or under-represented and low-moderate income populations.

The major problem in San Francisco is housing. The city, bounded by water on three sides, has just forty-nine square miles, a tiny valley. San Francisco is also rapidly becoming a city of single professional people – thirty per cent of the population. When couples started to move out into the suburbs to raise their families people assumed that this would take care of the housing problem, but they were replaced by single professionals. Blacks can no longer afford to live there because of the redevelopment and are going back over to the East Bay or San Mateo County. Because of the lack of space, San Francisco has the highest residential real estate rate in America. And how many people dream of living one day in those little boxes on the hillside made out of stucco or in the ornate, gingerbread Victorian homes with their bay windows stretched like sails in the wind?

Drugs are a serious problem, alcohol still remains an immense problem not only among the street people but across the city. Jobs are a problem like everywhere else, no longer confined to the unskilled. Highly skilled people who have been employed at pretty high income levels have been laid off. Calvary Presbyterian church – the 'cathedral' of the Presbyterians – has started a support group for management people and executives who have lost their jobs. Elsewhere in the city, support-groups for engineers in the same situation exist. The couple tells me that in the little church with which they co-operate, Seventh Avenue Presbyterian, a woman recently stood up talking about the prices of mortgages. She said that her grandson had been laid off and that he can't pay on unemployment an eleven hundred dollar a month mortgage and he certainly would lose his house.

The mental health problem seen from Tenderloin is one of the most serious problems, partly because so many people come to San Francisco at the end of their rope and partly because choices have been made on all levels to cut back, to cut back and to cut back on mental health services. The intern tells about a co-leader in the Tenderloin Ministry who has been himself a street person and a transvestite and who has been into drugs and alcohol. At the crisis in his life he was looking for psychiatric care but there just wasn't anything; if you finally find a mental health clinic you end up with a prescription to keep you going with chemicals. Middle-class and upper-class residents are angry because they feel the streets have been taken over by the crazies and criminals.

The couple thinks that it makes sense to continue to build up congregations because some people will continue to identify with them. But they think that other options have to be offered too. They have started house churches, small 'face-to-face groups' to 'do' and to 'be' the Good News. Members meet in homes in a non-threatening atmosphere and work through doubts, questions and personal identity problems as well as learning how to minister to each other. The Young Adult Network also offers retreats, and a covenant community is evolving. They are trying to develop a volunteer corps from suburban churches to do ministry in the city to help on a one-to-one basis and to listen. On Seventh Avenue they operate a coffee house where students from San Francisco State University or people from the gay/ lesbian community discuss issues like 'Inner Quest: Journalizing', 'The moods on college campuses across the country' or Bible study. They have developed a Tenderloin ministry in the hotels, at the Chateau Agape, a board and care home for mental patients. They encourage seminarians from the Pacific School of Religion to work with them, next to the financial district, among retired people, transients and refugees; the students are invited to learn a way of living out their education and applying it in a setting integrating it all – spiritual growth, problems of society, urban ministry, academic studies. Such a year is not meant to be a 'plunge', going in and coming right back out of it, but rather its antithesis: a 'mergence' experience in so far as

95

urban ministry is also a model for beyond the city. I also like the way the Young Adult Network is co-operating with Seventh Avenue Presbyterian church. The congregation had declined, and the Network needed a connection with a parish church as complement to the house church format as well as a place for larger gatherings in a young adult neighbourhood. A co-operative ministry allowing mutual influence and enrichment was worked out. Some of the underlying visions are 'to build bridges between middle-class church communities and marginalized people in the city, to effect reconciliation between the parish and the unchurched, to combine a high-risk, non-traditional, evangelistic ministry with a stable parish church'. One of their aims is also to develop models and intentional communities where people support one another in ministry – ecumenically, rooted in the life of the poor, inclusive with regard to all people usually excluded, so clearly of Christ that the ministry doesn't threaten any more but opens up ways of reconciliation – so that they can be developed elsewhere around the country.

My friends think that the churches in the Bay Area are very much into the corporation mentality. Battles have taken place in the Presbyterian church about the question of whether management methods should be taken over from corporate America, with the organizational style, a way of evaluating people so that you can assess this or that ministry as having so many more points than this ministry over here and pay according to the results. There are people who are pushing this, saying that if the Church is going to survive it has to adapt to modern life. On the other hand, intentional communities are struggling because they have no models to follow. How to develop new ways? They have tried some things with semi-success along those lines. Where it breaks down is at the point of economics. When they really talked about pooling their resources, they found themselves so influenced by the American way of life that they didn't know how to do that. 'We were too afraid.'

Churches dying? irrelevant to the world? hanging on to the family model in a society of divorce and new life styles? taking exclusive stands against gay people and only trying to keep their own institutions going? 'What we are experiencing now in a kind of spiritual rebirth is the discovery that the self is not enough.' The couple thinks there is now a search for something that is transcendent. The Churches apparently are not sufficiently fascinating, are too coloured by a certain culture and middle-class mentality and don't represent a hope for people who are at the end of the discovery of themselves. What could the Church become?

Traditionally, San Francisco has been seen as the place where you come to be reborn, a place to change your life where the Golden Gate and the wide open arms of St Francis welcome you. With all the Asians around and the East-West learning centres and the mysticism in the air, one wonders if this should not be the place where one day reconciliation between East and West could be explored, here where the great rocks are opened to the opportunities of the Orient and where the sun goes down outside the Golden Gate. The place is so beautiful that it must have been meant for adoration, contemplation, praise and prayer, searching for the infinite God ....

A cathedral of blessing hands

I'm in the subway on the way to a charismatic prayer group in the Northeast part of Philadelphia. A long ride, three-quarters of an hour. Someone will recognize me by the book I'm carrying under my arm, then a twenty-minute ride down spacious Roosevelt Boulevard (twelve lanes!). The man who meets me begins a no-holds-barred spiritual conversation so quickly that I ask him instead to explain to me the buildings we are passing. But his story touches me, his conversion from the usual muddle of a middle-aged man to this obsession with the Spirit.

I'm welcomed by a Franciscan. He has something maternal about him, a by-product of the spiritual life, no doubt. As I am somewhat nervous, all told, about whether I am up to the mark or not, the Churchill-like cigar resting in his mouth reassures me. A charismatic that smokes!

The pastor didn't like them, he tells me, so they have to meet in the church basement, and on top of it all no Eucharist. He doesn't like to see hands waving in the air in his church. But two hundred people are already there and from the loudspeakers music is blasting.

First those who lead the meeting pray among themselves, each one's arms around the shoulders of their neighbour. I hum along as best I can, but it's not quite speaking in tongues, yet. The Franciscan proposes that I lead the entire evening's prayer, but that's too much to ask: I'll say a few words at the end. All at once he asks me if I speak in tongues. Watch out now, I commit our Community by my answer. What can I say that is reasonably clear? That so often in the course of a day I hear the murmur of desire rise towards the heights of God? That I constantly hear in my heart the *cantus firmus* of the Spirit? Oh yes, I say, in the *Kyrie* at Taizé, in that flight of voices that raises mountains of crosses and of misery. And then, too, (the argument from authority) Cardinal Suenens told us that we are all charismatics. The Franciscan quickly realizes that we aren't talking about the same tongues, and I tell myself that I'd better shut up for a while so as not to disappoint him.

I am in the circle at the centre of the assembly. The participants are simple people, a man with sailor's tattoos on his arm, a young man, no doubt a mechanic, who seems like he just got out from under a car, women of all ages and all stripes, men – always with one hand discretely lifted as a sign of blessing and lips that move to the rhythm of the prayers.

We sing a lot; sometimes I know the melodies, in any case the band is louder than we are. There is beauty in the gestures of those praying, more varied than one might think; there is a longing in those arms elevated like a cathedral. I am still afraid of not being considered adequate, but I already feel a part of the humming, which comes together to form an astonishing harmony, and in the movements which are at the same time discreet and exuberant.

It's an exuberance which seems unconscious and which liberates you from suspicion and a critical eye, at least for a few minutes. The peace on their faces is real – so it's up to me to enter into their dance.

Some go up to the mike and speak of their visions, with no psychological detours. God speaks directly, and with such a pedagogical tone. But it concerns their real life, far from the world of illusions: family quarrels, sick friends, the refusal of God. All at once something moves me: I see the faces, one after another, of the people who live in our neighbourhood in New York, but more intensely than in reality, and I am aghast at their suffering. Then I see the brothers in the fraternity praying with great tenderness around the icon of the Cross and I see rays of light going from them to the others and the faces of the neighbourhood –dwellers become relaxed and peaceful.

A man gets up and say that we have all come here this evening with cares and worries. There are people here with worries that go from one to ten. One stands for an average worry in day-to-day life; ten means you don't think you'll get through the night. All at once he asks: who has ten? A few hands are raised, an old woman among others, sobbing. Right away we all turn around on our seats, we extend our right hand toward her and we pray out loud, our humming restores to that woman the promised harmony. Who has nine? And so on down the line.

Then it's my turn to speak. I spend a long time explaining the prayer around the cross, trying to adapt myself to their style of spiritual teaching as much as I can. Really, I am preaching to myself!

Surprisingly, they decide to pray for me. Hands are laid upon me and hands are raised throughout the church. A prayer for the gift of wisdom, that I allow my still untapped gifts to open up, that rivers of life may pass from my heart to the hearts of others .... I've forgotten the rest; the prayer went on and on.

But the music has already begun blasting again. One person is still praying with another sitting on the steps outside the door.

I find the Franciscan again. He has relit his cigar. On the way to the car, a priest stops me a moment to tell me of all God's promises. Let's go, I say to myself, to leave on the right foot.

My driver (all the way back to the house!) insists on rubbing oil on my hands and my forehead. I forgot the theory behind it, but I thought of Aaron's beard and of my host who was waiting at the house. He drove well and fast, and to my mind that excused him for the excess of spirituality he exuded. But I'm sure he was praying for me during the whole long ride back home.

I tell my host: I feel utterly relaxed. I spent an evening on the other side of the river.

St Joseph the Worker's impossible dreams

In the fifties, when segregation in Louisiana was still very strong, black Catholics in Amesville, Jefferson Parish purchased a piece of property on the corner of Ames Boulevard and a drainage ditch (later to become the Westbank Expressway). St Joseph the Worker was an almost totally Italian parish, and the blacks felt they needed a place to gather as a Christian community. They went to see Archbishop Rummel asking him for permission to become a parish. Archbishop Joseph Francis Rummel had, from the day he arrived in New Orleans, the insight that the Church should be a sign of interracial unity. In 1953 he had given directives: 'Ever mindful, therefore, of the basic truth that our coloured Catholic brethren share with us the same spiritual life and destiny, the same membership in the Mystical Body of Christ, the same dependence on the Word of God, the participation in the sacraments, especially the

100

most Holy Eucharist, the same need of moral and social encouragement, let there be no further discrimination, but they should not be harassed when they attend services in any parish church or mission, or when they apply for membership in parish organizations.' The Archbishop consequently told the black people from Amesville – the area nowadays is called Marrero – that the Church would not build a black church but that they were invited to be part of St Joseph the Worker. The blacks agreed and gave the property over to St Joseph the Worker. But the integration in the parish was far away. They had to sit in the back pews or to stand; the parish organizations were for white people only. In 1959 two black teenagers sat up front in the 'white section' at a Sunday morning Mass. Terrible emotion. The ushers ordered them to move. On another Sunday one usher blocked the path of a black woman, showing a gun. There was even more violence in 1962 over the integration of the school, picketing and bomb threats. The black priest – there are only two native diocesan black priests in the archdiocese – who tells me about those painful events assures me that the parish is still dealing with this recent history but that they have survived and somehow overcome the wounds of that time. The people have realized 'the deep-down prejudices, we have reached bottom'. People have been hurt and kept down but that very experience has made the parish different, more attentive to the needs of other groups that are oppressed today, more conscious of what is necessary to serve the people. Today the parishioners try to bring about healing, growth, understanding.

Five years ago the parish started to dream about a new church building. In the meantime the Westbank Expressway had been built. MacDonald's offered to purchase the piece of property the blacks of Amesville had once bought for fifteen thousand dollars through fund-raising, bazaars and collections. MacDonald's bought the land for 200,000 dollars. This money was used as seed money to build the new church. So the black people in the fifties were instrumental in laying the foundations of church life in this area over against harsh resistances. The old church was not demolished but sold to a Baptist congregation. It must have been something the day the trucks came and rolled the church ten blocks away. The media called it an 'ecumenical movement'.

A surprising parish, St Joseph the Worker. First of all, the parish ministry is led by a team of two priests, seven religious women and a laywoman. In this archdiocese only a very few parishes could say that they have a team ministry. Each person on the team is responsible for a whole area of ministry. Each one is accountable to the pastor, not to somebody else. At their weekly meeting, we are sitting in the rectory around the table. A St Joseph Sister works with the senior citizens, the bereaved families and the sick. Lay Eucharistic ministers bring communion from the Sunday Mass to the shut-ins. If there is a death in the parish, the Good Shepherd Ministry says the rosaries at the wake, cooks a hot meal for the family on the day of the funeral, prepares the memorial Mass for the following Sunday, prints prayer cards and follows up with visits to the family. A second Sister works, as she says, 'with the Kingdom inheritors'. Anyone who knocks on the door and says he or she is in need is a Kingdom inheritor. It helps her to see her own ministry not as a work done for them but as a work *with* them, aimed at the development of people. She works in the Social Apostolate centre – the salaries for three and a half workers come from the Archbishop's appeal but the funding for the direct services come from the parish tithing. They have a food co-op. Through the bulletin the congregation is educated concerning issues like the death penalty, the nuclear arms race, the Nestlé boycott, the MX missile. Petitions are signed, letters are sent to the Congressman. Some years ago the parish was involved in some community organizing for a neighbourhood clean-up and for recreation programmes in the community. A third Sister does all the public relations work. One of their aims is to involve as many parishioners as possible in a ministry. Her task is to get the knowledge about the different ministries to the people so that they can be known and appreciated.

In this parish four hundred people are involved in some ministry, in visiting the sick, in leading Bible study groups, in giving communion, witnessing on Sunday, singing in one of the four choirs, as lector, in social justice, working with the poor or the bereaved, teaching religion, in the art ministry. There are fifty items on a list of ministries. This leadership development allows a greater sense of ownership and changes the image of the congregation from a parish on the receiving end and a clergy giving directives to a gradual acceptance of multiple lay ministries enabled by a team ministry. More and more the parish team understands its role as ministering to the ministers so that lay leaders in the parish image themselves as the primary ministers of the parish. The Archdiocese is contemplating a decision to limit the term of service for a pastor to eight years and for an associate to four years; Sisters in the future will be less available, less numerous or will be called to other tasks. The parish team therefore prepares the parish for the time to come to be more confident in its own capacities to minister. Twelve married couples already assume marriage preparation for engaged couples. Forty lay ministers have been trained to visit the sick.

The area was originally an Italian settlement. French people moved in after the Second World War, as well as a large number of black families. Today the area is fifty per cent black, fifty per cent white. It is designated as a poverty area. A federal housing project is located in the area. The men work on the shipyards along the river or in a factory for building material; there are some teachers. The older families especially are traditional; a statue of the Blessed Mother stands in front of their house, and they are very attached to the devotion to the saints. All the Masses are culturally distinct, although those who attend are somehow mixed. The two black gospel music Masses attract eighty per cent blacks, and at the Saturday evening 'white' Mass not only older people are present.

Two other women at the table are in charge of the racially mixed school. The black priest is very active in the National Black Clergy and Sisters Caucus; when he is at home he focuses on the music ministry, especially on the black gospel music. His conviction is that the Church in America does not look at the black American as if they have something to offer to the Church. The Church offers services to the blacks but is not with them, doesn't appreciate their gifts; the Church in general is not respectful of the distinctive backgrounds of the white and black people. The Church does not enrich herself with the blacks' sense of family, of forgiveness, of survival. At St Joseph the Worker, however, the people deal with this tension. The pastor of this integrated parish lights up when he speaks about the blacks in his congregation. He admires their gift of endurance, the way they carry the burdens of life, the family tragedies, the economic difficulties, the prejudices. He admires their deeply inborn religious sense. In the parish the blacks have the possibility of expressing themselves freely and of approaching life with a sense of totality. The other staff members work with the separated and the divorced, the parish council, marriage annulment, a parish census. There is no consistent work together with the Lutheran church and the fifteen small Baptist black churches.

'Dreaming' is a word that comes up all the time in the conversation. 'We dream up things, and we try it.' The team has received a training from the Management Design Inc in Cincinnati. This ecumenical group composed of priests, ministers and religious, some of them highly skilled in management, felt a decade ago that management groups in the country were not adequately equipped to enable church management because church groups in their opinion come out of a deep faith commitment and management groups couldn't get down into that depth. So they devised an organization development for churches. Parishes in New Orleans struggling with their parish councils – either considering their role as insignificant or making decisions that traditionally had been prerogatives of the clergy – contracted with the MDI to put on a training programme for six weekends. The basic idea of the MDI is to show the deepest dreams, the aspirations, the hopes, the common memory people have, the experiences they went through together and their expression in symbols and celebrations. For a person individually as well as for a group they consider such a historicizing, dreaming-type process, reflecting on the journey of a parish community, very important in order to touch the deep level of life. Only when those dreams are articulated is it possible to define goals and finally to build programmes. Their point is that most often parishes limit themselves to formulating programmes and don't go down into the myth life of the group, to gain an in-depth vision.

At St Joseph the Worker some years ago the team invited the congregation to share their dreams for the future of the parish. People were asked to complete on paper the following statement: 'It would be wonderful and a great blessing for our parish if some day. . .'. Many took part in it, especially the black youth. Spiritual renewal came first; that the poor would be cared for; that we love one another; racial and social justice; that we learn more about the Bible; that there be no more financial troubles . . . . The clergy was setting all the goals helped by a few suggestions from the parish. The most important dreams – they call them 'impossible dreams' – were circled, indicating the identity of the parish. Some of them read: 'Everyone that left the church would return', 'Everyone of us would come to know the Lord Jesus and give him first place in our hearts', 'Our Sunday celebrations would be the highlight of everyone's week because they understood deep within why they came to church'. . . . While the congregation does the dreaming, is responsible for articulating the myth and the deepest values, a parish assembly of a hundred people that meets each year translates those basic dreams into goals. They address the question: what would it be like for our parish, if by this time next year we began to attain this or that goal? The parish council then decides objectives for each goal, and the parish team develops programmes, and reports back to the congregation. The programmes nurture the congregation again as they prepare to set new goals. It sounds like a heavy structure but in reality the whole process is smooth, groups interact, the preaching influences the different steps and the overall result is a greater sense of belonging and enthusiasm.

Over the years the parish council has decided to give a portion of the income from offerings to the poor. It comes to ten per cent. Four per cent goes to missions that were adopted, in Zambia, Mexico and Guatemala, one per cent goes to the school to help poor families to pay for tuition, five per cent goes directly to the poor in the community. Families are also asked to take part in a tithing of ten per cent, symbolizing that all we have is from God and that we are invited to give back to him our whole life. Although the parish is mainly composed of people with low or moderate incomes, a lot of parishioners have made far-reaching decisions and commitments in this field.

Next Sunday is Prayer Commitment Sunday. People are invited to recommit themselves to a life of closer union to the Lord. In a brochure possibilities for prayer are indicated: 'No home is too small or too simple to become a sacred place of prayer. As a first step, each person or family may select a special place of prayer. This can be a table or a corner of a room or a spot near the religious symbol such as a candle, a cross, a Bible, a statue or picture.' They are asked to fill out a prayer commitment form. At the offertory of the Mass those who commit themselves are invited to come forward, to have a sign of the cross made on their forehead. In entering the church, I'm impressed by the silence and the intense listening. Fifty choir members enter and stand behind the altar during the Eucharist. The priest stands in front of the clapping and rocking choir like a choreographer directing his dancers. Inner joy shines on their faces. The choir joins the assembly for the greeting of peace and mounts again towards the altar full of reverence and inner abandonment for communion. The priest holds up a crystal plate covered by an immaculately white cloth and later a large brandy bowl with a spout. The altar bread is homemade. A little girl receives a benediction. A woman takes the communion for the sick. The catechumens have been sent out of the church until they will be admitted to the Eucharist at Easter. All the races are present. Mothers with young children stand in a large 'cry room'. The church is filled with prayer. What a beautiful ministry, to be a priest among people who pray: 'Bless me with your abounding love as I promise to be your friend, servant and holy minister'.

What heaven is like, heard in Harlem

I walked through Harlem with the senior minister of the Metropolitan Community United Methodist Church. We were part of a crowd of several hundred people, and we stopped at Memorial Baptist church for a brief prayer in the middle of their service, then continued through Morningside Park up to St John the Divine. The senior minister was dressed in his ecclesiastical vestments, a majestic presence of salvation on the dilapidated streets of Harlem. Some black preachers have a way of speaking you can feel more than that you understand, like those actors who are able to make their audience believe that they are making sense while they deliberately speak nonsense syllables, only dropping a recognizable expression from time to time. The language of the Spirit must be something like that: humanly speaking, a rigmarole of gutturals interspersed with an occasional vowel provoking our aha's because finally we are able to look back and understand what the gutturals meant. In the voice of the senior minister an overtone of joy suddenly breaks in; he is still pronouncing words but on a wavelength that the intelligence can no longer grasp – only the soul can hear. Then suddenly his voice emits, from within, a perfectly intelligible line that explains what preceded it by enlightening you.

We were talking about the psychological and sociological knowledge he had acquired. He threw it out of the window because – and here comes in that other voice out of the depths – *Christ can redeem.* He spoke about the two thousand, eight hundred youngsters he got into a college or university, the fifty-six ordained ministers who came out of his last two parishes and the hundred and twenty-nine members of the two youth gangs he worked with in the Bronx. His life, he says, is devoted to a redemptive process for the total personality which means to be born again, to be transformed by the renewal of the mind, to acquire a new set of values, another base from which to think. He quotes Kierkegaard saying that you come to the place where you stand naked before God and acknowledge that God has a greater mind than we have. Young people are hungry for the spiritual dimension, their minds have to be captured for Christ because to fit into the universal pattern of creation is what life is all about. So the young people who are hustling, standing around on Times Square or in Harlem, reached, touched, rehabilitated, are taken to a seminar on Thursdays. He does not go out to show how spiritual he is but *you look at the person where they are,* where they are hurt and then you offer them the greatness of life that comes from God. The whole thing is to bring the person up to where they can see that the Church is the body of Christ. They have to be a part of the caring fellowship of love and understanding. They become a part of what you are through Jesus Christ. Jesus never condemned anybody. We don't have to say: you ought not ... but here is *what you can become.* Everybody has some sense of grace in him or her. The Church must have that in mind. Divisions wrecked the Christian Church. There is no community with one another. Individualism is the sorry history of depicting Christ on a false base; what we really have to be is the Body of Christ.

In the seminar the disciplines of humankind are studied, the natural and the behavioural sciences, psychology and ethics, logic and philosophy to reflect upon our stands in society, epistemology and theology: how does God deal with the world? What is spiritual? How do we get the idea of the Holy? Why is love better than anything else? What makes you able to do that? Later in the seminar they get beyond their own psyche and learn about the mind which was in the Lord Jesus Christ. And then they pray: Thy kingdom come on earth as it is in heaven. Heaven always takes care of itself but we are instruments in His hands, to be used by Him so that the will of God be done in this world. *Christ came to show us what heaven was like and what the world could be.* This is the Church, and therefore we have to *rise above* the rigid, legalistic, pharisaical things in each church that keep us apart and that keep us from enjoying the greatness with one another. In the early Church Christians loved one another. How are we going to do that today? The choice of which denomination is better should not have to be made by those who are searching for God. We should become instruments to show Christ revealed in the flesh. Black Muslims or Jews have a wonderful religion but they have prescriptions by principle of law. You have to fit into something that is not human. You read a book, you look at the law – it has to become you, you must become like this, and you can't do it. But Paul says that Christ wherever we go, be it on the lowest depths or to the very gates of hell, He has been there too. It is love. We are instruments of that love. *Love is the extension of the Godliness in us* to others, sometimes by sacrificing our whole mind, not doing what we would like to do but doing what we are called to do. This does not enrich only the others but our life as well, because we share what has been so wonderful and magnificent in our redemption. We might have to suffer but *Jesus is always standing among us.* People are punishing themselves by not working with the universal plan of God, which always is positive. If we go in other directions, it is like swimming up the stream in a swift current, it is like going against the laws of grammar, you can't do it. God is doing it. It is *the Father's good pleasure to give you the Kingdom.*

One day, the minister walked on Times Square. His method was to make himself a target, then to see why this person was here, first to confront the evil wherever it was, prostitution, drugs, violence. So he was going up Eighth Avenue. A girl approached him: do you want to go out? He said: Yes, and he stopped and engaged her in a conversation. What does it cost? As a matter of fact he was on his way to the hospital on 50th St. So he said he would be back in half an hour and he promised to give her the money for her proposition. He came back and gave her the money but he said: go home now. I would like to meet you, he said; here is my phone number, let's have lunch. The girl was confused and said she had never met anybody like him. He said: Yes, you have never met *me.* He smiled and set up a date with her to meet at a restaurant. She came from Minnesota. They talked together. He asked: What would you like to be other than an actress? She said she had been thinking about becoming a teacher. Why don't you be a teacher? Well, you see me, I can't. Why? I have no resources, I have a pimp, I have no place to stay, I have no money to go to school, I have no job. But at each problem she mentioned he said that he could handle that, and he did. She worked as a waitress, she went to a college for teachers, she married and she has a fine family. Last week he had lunch with one of the girls of the gang in the Bronx who is now a professor of psychology on the West Coast. *Go in the name of Jesus and show that He is alive in our lives.*

The minister's first longing had been to become a medical doctor. Grade school in Mississippi was held from the first grade to the eighth grade in one room, with one teacher. Not only was the school system segregated but the State

110

almost threw the blacks out of the school system, and they had their classes in the church. Church and school were the same because the board of supervisors of the county didn't furnish school buildings for blacks at that time. The community people finally built another school building but they had to do it themselves, without tax money. Only the teacher was furnished at a very low salary, not comparable with the white teachers. When he finished grade school there was no high school for blacks in the county, only a big white high school to where the white kids were bussed in. So he left the State at the age of thirteen for Monroe, Louisiana. Later he went to a junior college at the Southern Christian Institute that was founded in the meantime in Mississippi. Financially a lady helped him to study at the university. But during all that time his mind was set on becoming a doctor. However, he changed in three days. On Sunday somebody had spoken to him about commitment, and he had almost laughed. But Tuesday night in bed he could not sleep. He heard a loud noise. Usually, he never woke up at night. Now he wondered what this noise was. He got up, got out of bed and went to see if some of the other people in the house were awake but they were sleeping. He was awake, it was not a dream. He really had a vision, a vision of Christ, and the vision was of such a nature that he knew he had to go into the ministry. 'From then on my whole life has been spent in that direction.'

In September, his month of vacation, he walks in the garden he has upstate, writes most of his sermons there, composes cantatas; he finds sustenance in being creative. What keeps him going? *You must see God as wonderful. My security is really not found in the world.* He sings: What a friend we have in Jesus. And he looks like he did thirty years ago.

Arriving at St John the Divine and leaving him after our common pilgrimage through Morningside Park, I thought a man like him, like Henoch, walks with God.

5

Struggling for a Reconciled Church

The laughter in the joke at St John the Divine
The deanery on the grounds of the New York City's
Episcopal Cathedral, St John the Divine, looks like an
aristocratic Greenwich home which has strayed to the edge
of Harlem – a small remnant of the glorious history of
Morningside Heights. In the house every quarter of an hour
one hears the Cathedral chimes, recalling the medieval
scene of pilgrims lost in a forest who find their path by
following the sound waves of a carillon. Even the noise of
the crazily cruising cars on Amsterdam Avenue is sifted and
immobilized in the silence of a house where art and
artlessness hold hands trying to convince you of another
world that transcends the shameless shape to which Harlem
is fallen. Next to me stands a totally abstract glass sculpture
in the shape of a lotus.

I remember I had asked the Dean a lot of questions when
I arrived the first time in New York years ago. At that time
he saw a wonderful 'new humility' in the churches. His
theory was that the Church was finally recognizing its
institutionality and its connections to the power structures
of society. Apparently a time of reformation was beginning
to dawn. It is impressive indeed that throughout history the
Church has at regular intervals been challenged in its
bureaucracy, its richness, its property and its decision-
making. Mostly this began and ended *within* the Church,
the exception being the Reformation in the sixteenth
century. Purists, dissidents, reformers, prophets, preachers
and mystics have again and again shaken the tree of the
Church, dethroned institutional legitimacy before recognizing that no power seems to be strong enough to ruin the ever

new emerging institutional drive. The Dean thought at that time that it was becoming clearer and clearer that 'although the body of the Church will wither, Jesus is risen from the dead'. The institutional cover of the Church was opposed to the 'new life', found in strange and unexpected places. He saw 'all sorts of sparks of wonderful new life in the Church' out of reach of institutional labels. He didn't exclude the structures – how can you be a Dean without having to work in and with them from morning to night? – but his point was that the religious task was to make New York hopeful, to be open, to welcome the new, seeing it not as a threat but as a promise. 'You must build your church where the people are and where the need is. As opposed to saying that the church is simply here and the people are going to come to it ... because they don't.' Summarizing our conversations of five years ago, I remember the distinction he made between the Church as the Body of Christ present among the 'least of these my brethren', in the hearts of the faithful and the suffering, and the Church constantly tempted to hypostatize itself and to become the structure apart from the people. The latter wants to get its steeple with the heat on, the taxes paid, with the power game and the inertia of every institution, dealing first with its own internal problems that finally get the upper hand and becoming predatory on everything around it. He felt that the new humility consisted in recognizing that.

Today his opinions seem even more radical. His hope for the Church in the future is that 'it will disappear'. He means the 'clubby' Church, the organization perhaps useful in terms of projects but fundamentally betraying what the Church is called to be in the life of the people. For him the Church is like the 'laughter in the joke', it is a dimension, a depth of living, a way of seeing things, an understanding of life and death and resurrection, a way of giving thanks. 'Every time I see that name church, I want to run in the opposite direction.' Church reminds him of 'programmatic doings', of Christians walking around with big banners saying that the Church is doing things, pushing its public relations while the real Church is a point of view that enables you to live, and to join others who have the same point of view, it is the capacity to see the glory in all creation, including suffering and distress. It is expressed in liturgy, in mystical prayer, and in the service of people, doing things wherever they are needed, out of whatever references, labelled or not. Millions of things need to be done in New York and it's fine to organize things – St John the Divine's doings are numerous – if only it could be done without names and badges, without conditions and comparisons, without judging and counting, above all without excluding. The Church at work, he says, are the people who are actually doing Christ's work today, who are serving the suffering, the dying, the bleeding, who rejoice with the joyful, who 'get off their ass' and do something. Christ is doing it, it doesn't depend on the self-consciousness of people who believe in Him and therefore decide to act. No name-tags: Buddhists or Muslims or anybody else can do Christ's work perfectly well. There is no need to belong to that sociological entity called church to do things in Christ's spirit, no need of a confessing self-consciousness to be part of what the Church really is: 'Resurrection unleashed'.

He can't stand that other Church any more. 'As it is now, the Church is a kind of an Antichrist.' He would like to get rid of that Church that doesn't recognize the world as the icon of the Kingdom, that doesn't see the world with the people as the Kingdom because the Spirit is at work there in them. Christians are people like all the others except that they have a consciousness of what is happening; but they don't need to go around saying: the Church is doing it. The main hubris of the Church is to exclude people, to label God's creation clean as opposed to dirty, to judge, to make rules about what we are supposed to do or not, to enter into 'devilish' notions of good and false, true and bad. 'Everything that's good is for cheers, don't bother who did it.' He has never felt more and more Christian while becoming

114

increasingly anti-Church. The Church is saying what Christ is doing and what He is not doing but we are not supposed to do that. All the good things, in other religions, among non-Christians – Christ is behind it. Would He be doing something less? We are only supposed to be fed. Here He is, dying on the Cross, giving up His body and blood, for everybody, for the world. 'Or would it be for some kosher club?' If it was given for the world, then it is for everybody. The Dean is opposed to the notion of 'open communion', which implies that it is not for everybody, as if something could be possibly closed again. Curiously he calls this limitation of God's grace 'heresy', 'that's Antichrist', words one wouldn't expect in the mouth of someone who calls himself a 'universalist'. Is he not excluding a large part of the church people and, in a certain sense, a large part of his own ministry? Upset because of the exclusions, one tends to exclude in turn those who have wounded us. But in listening to him I like to think that he uses that strong language in order to make clearer the point he is struggling with: how to incarnate in the necessary, visible structures the width, the breadth and the depth of Christ's presence in every human being, in history and in the universe?

In spite of the planned towers of the Cathedral, the running of the place, the conflicts and the judgements, how to be a leaven on that artistic Upper West Side, as neighbours of black Harlem and with the claim, however it is understood, to be the international Cathedral of New York? The Cathedral may be empty, the events may seem to some syncretistic or appear to turn that space into a music hall or a town hall, with ambassadors preaching and aerialists attracting the attention on the front page of the New York Times – I'm impressed by his vision of the crucified and risen Christ who is there whether we acknowledge Him or not, feeding everybody with the bread of life, of Christ who plants seeds of His Kingdom in unexpected places, and especially through art, bringing about the transfiguration of all those people and all those places around us. If the Dean says to me that 'anything less than that verges on, no, *is* heresy' and that 'the way the Church operates is total heresy, based on exclusion, based on a distinction which can't be', I don't see in it so much the disappointment of a man in the fire of criticisms who in spite of that manages to translate his insights into the thousand projects of St John the Divine, but rather the negative and, I think, unilateral expression of an extreme generosity, based on Christ's, maybe impossible to enflesh in the down-to-earth realities of church bodies but certainly prophetic.

A painting I look at behind the Dean's shoulders says it all to me: six feet square, it probably represents the rising of the sun, with dark brownish earth colours overshadowed by a great deal of orange and yellow, and some mauve, blue-green, blue. The orange and the yellow seem to say something about the utmost joy of abandoning oneself to the mystery of the holy, they seem to cross over all the impediments on the way, yet without annihilating them but rather integrating and going beyond them. The Dean got it from a friend on the day the godfather of his children killed himself in a mental hospital in Paris. Art for him is a fundamental mode of sacred communication; the arts, whether visual or performing, are the hands, the feet, the eyes and the voice through which religion has to express itself. Art and religion are in a sisterly relationship in that they both evoke what is transcendent in life. I like to imagine that this painting with its silent joy sometimes rescues the day of a Dean.

Concerts of prayer at Moody Bible Institute
Like in all seminaries and theological schools, prayer is a problem at Moody Bible Institute. An older student who was a serviceman in Hawaii before his conversion speaks to me about the necessity of a revival on the campus. I am surprised to hear that. I admire those hundreds of students who have chosen this school and who I see walking from

116

class to class, from Jeremiah to evangelism, with the Bible in their hands or under their arm, trying to live up to the high moral standards of this whole environment. Lively people who could take it easy and plunge themselves into the beauty of this world are tormenting themselves because one day they have seen a glimpse of God and since then they have wanted to let him take over all the decisions of life, love, future, work, fellowship and happiness. Many of them will go overseas to witness and to communicate the invisible reality of Christ they have one day entered into without knowing what was happening. I admire God's walk with these students and would think that God in his goodness prays enough with them, in their hearts, so that in the meantime they can do some theology and finish the school term quickly and leave behind all that anxiety. But the serviceman says that the statistics are alarming. On campus the students have the opportunity to attend a prayer meeting for different areas of the world from Monday through Thursday from 6 to 7 pm. There is a China prayer group, one for Asia, one for Europe (France is considered as one of the most secularized countries where nobody goes to church any more . . .). But out of a total of 1350 students, only eighty are involved in those groups. Somebody had to take on the concern for prayer. The ex-serviceman ran for this office – unopposed – and was elected by the students. He criticizes the fact that at Moody, as in other Bible colleges, prayer is not taught at all. Only the Personal Evangelism Course, in which faith is shared and some topics of discipleship are discussed, touches occasionally on the theme of prayer.

Last Friday night he had gathered a hundred students for a 'concert of prayer', a term that comes down the ages from Jonathan Edwards. The need was felt to band together for longer periods of time in prayer. They pattern it after the concerts of prayer in the 1700s that resulted in the Great Awakening. The other purpose is to express the desire of their hearts that the Body of Christ be united. A concert

117

means several instruments blending, sounds coming together to make beautiful music. That is their desire in prayer: that a unified desire for prayer be brought to the Body of Christ in Chicago, that an awakening take place, a seeking of Christ, a revival. A concert of prayer lasts two hours. At the start a man explains for ten minutes how to pray specifically along the lines of revival and gives some instructions from the Word of God. He emphasizes that a concert is not a solo and that this prayer will be focused on revival, not so much in ourselves but in the Church, on a Christian revival in Chicago, also in the Christian communities around, whatever denominational affiliations they may have, a revival that would touch those who don't know Christ yet. Then he asks people in the audience to find three or four others sitting near them and to group together. After forty or forty-five minutes of personal prayer for the fullness of Christ in the local churches, during which individuals can stand up or speak out or sing a song whenever God leads them to do so, they come together in the small groups for five or ten minutes. Many are moved to tears and cry; 'God breaks many hearts'. Then again personal prayer for forty-five minutes, this time for the fulfilment of the 'great commission' and for revival worldwide. Before this concert of prayer, many students had committed themselves to a twenty-four hour prayer chain, from noon to noon, in which each one took half an hour to prepare for the concert of prayer. Concerts of prayer are taking place across the country as well. Mission teachers try to stir up a movement of prayer on the campuses, and some go from one campus to another, visit one city after another 'to seek the Lord' (they refer to Zech. 8.20–24).

Is there some vision of what this revival in the churches in Chicago will look like? The ex-serviceman says that God is in the process right now of teaching them what revival is and has moved several of them to begin reading, to feed their hearts about what God has done in the past in great revivals. The last great revival in the Western world seems

118

to have taken place in 1904–5 in Wales. In a period of six months, a hundred thousand people came to Christ, the churches had to be open twenty-four hours a day, the coal miners were so touched by the Gospel that they went from cursing and swearing to singing hymns of praise in the mines, Russian and Japanese seamen – who were at war – were touched by the outpouring of God's spirit and found peace. A revival will be preceded, sustained and held together by a movement of prayer. It is the waking up of the Church to what she has received in Christ, which ultimately would cause the Church to spill over into the world. It reminds me of the image of Ezekiel of the dead bones brought to life by the Spirit.

The ex-serviceman has a limited exposure to the local churches in Chicago. He went a couple of Sundays to Moody Bible Church, Fourth Presbyterian church and St Paul's Evangelical Lutheran church. But his heart was 'burdened', he felt no sense of worship, 'no desperation to get out the Gospel', no hunger and thirst for God, only a traditional formality, no enthusiasm for the things of God, although at Moody Church some revival on a small scale has taken place. Would it be a good idea, I ask, to have marches of repentance in the area, from cathedral to cathedral, to make manifest the suffering over the divisions among Christians? But for him reconciliation is a tricky word because of the danger that the truth would be damaged, that compromises would be made. The Catholic organization especially seems to him very far away, although there are individual Catholics who believe in being born again. He asks me if I have ever seen evangelical doctrinal viewpoints reconciled with the Catholic persuasion? In studying Church history he has noticed that at the time of the Reformation the Catholic Church declared all the Prot-estants heretics and he does not know how far we have come today from that point. Are Catholics ready to drop that line and to say that the others are not heretics but brothers and sisters in Christ? They need, in his opinion, to return to

119

biblical teaching, to the foundation of Scripture. Have Catholics come to that point? It is hard for him to know how far the Evangelicals should come in order to meet with Catholicism, and yet Holy Name Cathedral, strictly avoided, is next door. But he thinks that at the grassroots level a uniting of hearts can take place. On that level things that are not essential will drop out of the picture. Points of dispute will fade away, when the things that the Scripture holds as doctrinally true, important and right are embraced by all those involved in a revival. 'I can see that happening.'

How do I see ways for a revival to take place? Revival, for those who search for it, often means reconciliation with God. But reconciliation is a dynamic process; there is not authentic reconciliation in God if it does not lead to ways of becoming reconcilers in Church and society. Revival means also visiting others unknown to us, breaking down barriers, discovering sister-churches, organizing people in coalitions so that justice comes about. Rather than a church federation at the top, would a ministry of visits between sister-churches be a way of cutting through a traumatizing set of hitherto unmoved dividing lines? Is it too idealistic to envisage inter-racial, inter-ethnic teams of people with the full-time job of going day after day through the city, as messengers of unity and organizers of justice? Visits could not remain on the level of spiritual sharing. If spiritual sharing is real, it inevitably leads to a more total commitment that includes the search for the roots of peace. Would unemployed people be interested in such a ministry, ready for a profound preparation, willing to construct, in an often hidden way, in spite of thousands of frustrations, a new face of the Church that rediscovers its unity and that takes part in the struggle of the poor not only in their own area but throughout the whole city, relying upon innumerable people of hope who now, isolated, are devoured by all the demands they have to answer alone?

A few days later at the entrance of LaSalle Street Baptist church I meet a young woman who had seen me at MBI and who wants to explain some more. She is very outspoken. She didn't feel at ease at Fourth Presbyterian Church firstly for personal reasons, the service differs from her church at home in Buffalo, New York. She does not like the fact that all the people who go there are money-orientated. 'It is the church of the elite.' She also went to one of the social get-togethers on Sunday evening for young adults. She criticizes the fact that it was just a social gathering; the speaker missed the whole point of communication, because for someone whose Saviour is Christ there is an immediate bond and closeness with others who believe. 'They miss that. God was not in the conversation.' She misses in the churches the experience of God. She has a 'real block' with regard to churches with formal rituals 'where you do this and this and this' and where you can't pray. Although she comes from a Baptist home and her parents depend on God, 'also financially', she is a new Christian. As an art major she studied at a State school and got involved in partying, smoking, drinking and fun and lost her own identity. She couldn't put on an act before her parents and felt upset every night, not knowing if there was a God at all. She prayed that if God was there, He would show her that He could change her life. She was not happy. Then she decided to go to church for Easter and in entering the church she felt 'electric'. She knew that this presence of the Holy Spirit was real, that she had messed up her life, and that God could make her happy and turn her life around. She 'went up' and 'felt from black to white'. She became born-again. She says that she still has many questions, that she needs a Bible background and that as a student at Moody she is now struggling through all that doctrinal stuff. People think life must be easy at Moody, but Satan, she says, works there more than anywhere else. He pulls people away from Christ, discouraging them because of all the work you have to do. All the academic head knowledge somehow has to be converted in a 'daily walk with Christ'. Personally she needs verbal prayer, to hear herself saying her prayers, because her mind wanders so easily. At Moody there is no small chapel and it's hard to pray when your roommate is there. But she knows that prayer works, 'God honours those who pray'. She wants to 'conquer' the goals she had wanted to reach since her conversion. She has to get through the anxiety of all the work that has to be done. In the churches people never say that they need the personal relationship with Christ and need to let Him rule in their existence. She has the 'deep' feeling that the churches remain on the surface, especially the Catholics who 'work, work, work in order to get to heaven' and who have only 'empty reasons just to earn heaven', who need a priest for confession, remaining all week out of fellowship with Christ after having sinned and not seeing that you can pray yourself to God.

Students at Moody have a weekly ministry, either in a church or in a nursing home. She works with black kids. She would like later to work with Blacks or Latinos, or perhaps become a missionary in Europe. Each time she sees her cousins, they ask: What are you going to do when you get out? How are you going to make money? But she wants to depend totally on God, 'on my God'. She is not living just for life but for eternity. 'The world is going to end soon, the Lord will return, I am ready for that.'

And then she walks away, back to school, twenty years old, dancing in the street, looking at the fashions in the store windows because she likes nice clothing, a charming young person who loves God.

Listening to a Baptist sermon
I'm with a friend, listening to one of the Sunday sermons sent to me by the San Antonio Trinity Baptist tape ministry (I've been receiving one every week ever since I went there). In this week's sermon, the minister's point is that penitence is not a prerequisite for receiving God's love and forgiveness, as if we had to soften God's wrath or anger towards us, until he finally, reluctantly, agrees to accept us again.

Rather, penitence is the result of the inner perception that we are already immersed in God's unconditional love and forgiveness. This unconditional love is really his theme.

I'm fond of this kind of sermon, of its ambience and loftiness, like a hymn of your youth, heard in later years in a foreign country. You hear the breathless silence of the people, suddenly astonished in a kind of nostalgia about forgotten ideals. You feel welling up that murmuring desire to abandon yourself to the only reality, hidden in our lives, suddenly recognized in the glades of your inner obscurity.

The sermon is also remarkably expressed, alternately funny and moving. Why would we lessen our veneration for the glowing Gospel message by a puritanical reluctance to use rhetorical forms? America is a land of preachers, of stentorian amplifiers of an unheard secret. All that they need is to stand in the middle of a crowd, on a bench along the road or in the sculptured pulpits of neo-Gothic cathedrals, and there they go, pitching the ball to the batter, right at the heart, making people run on the roundabouts of life. I would be able to listen over and over again to the sounds of these sermons, whirling around you like leaves in the air, driven by the wind on zigzagging detours, until at the end the message sinks through the clouds of doubt and hesitancy into our very depths, and we are capable of wonder again.

But as I was listening lots of questions came to me. Does the reality of God's love express itself first and foremost in an individual and private experience, leading me right away beyond the depressive realities of evil in the world and in myself, in a personal enlightenment that lifts up my life? Or should it, in order to be true, first of all be woven into the texture of my life with others in society, over a long period of time? An instant experience? Or should it, in order to be authentic, lead me through the combats of life and society to the perspective of a transfiguration that includes all the others? How do I, within my individual consciousness, filled with doubt, deeply wounded by the sense of sin,

123

loneliness and loss assure myself of the truth of God's grace and love and forgiveness, in a way other than just by feeling it? And too, deep in myself I'm not alone but linked by a thousand threads to other people, entangled in a network of relationships which all together make up my life. How to receive God's promise in the midst of this communion?

The emphasis we place on one or the other alternatives depends a great deal on where we come from. My friend is saying that, if your sense of reality comes from connections, from connectedness with others, with the living and the dead, with other cultures and people (different from you in your own culture), then an experience however strong, moving, truthful that would leave you alone without relating yourself to others, would be for you an illusion. On the contrary, for people who are very much marked by the individualistic experience, who imagine themselves as separate from others, who come from a cultural context aimed at *you* instead of *us*, the reality is inside of themselves. There are people who feel they can change every relationship they have and still remain themselves; they can change church, husband, wife, job without really changing, because who they are is independent of all relationships, and their relationships are less than they are. Obviously, in an African tribe, people do not feel this way: if you have to leave the village, if you are expelled for whatever reason, you are considered and you consider yourself as dead. I have met women in Mathare Valley, a huge slum in Nairobi, who were expelled in that way, for sexual transgression, into the darkness of non-existence, out of the centre of the world which rests at the heart of the tribe's consciousness. At the opposite pole of this attitude you find the self-conscious experience of the individual, independent of his or her relationship with others, people, cultures, past and future, who accepts his or her personal Saviour in an instant. But our friendship, love, marriage or whatever bonds we have with people can never lead instantly to a commitment; to let another person into your life takes time. Is there not therefore a kind of romanticism in the belief that there will be suddenly a breakthrough in my life and that all I need is to say 'yes' and 'amen', to come forward and to decide to change my life? Or is this finally that amazing 'grace' that operates independently from us, that is simply already there as the supporting reality of all life in which we are immersed long before we become conscious of it?

I'm struggling with these questions. On the one hand I'm stirred by this sermon and I hear today in it a knock on the door – and I want to welcome Christ with open arms. On the other hand, I would expect the minister to say to me: listen, once you accept him, you are no longer an individual, you are no longer separate from others, however different they may be, you are now part of a larger body, part of one self, of the mystical body of Christ; find out the consequences of that.

Is this extreme individualism the result of the emphasis on partial aspects of the great and vast reality of God's grace that happened to all the reform movements throughout the history of Christianity? People refused the teachings of the Roman Catholic Church or the established Churches; they no longer found the truth of the Gospel in them and separated themselves (or were thrown out and persecuted) from the broader communion. Then they emphasized a few basic insights, making these insights the *sine qua non* without which no salvation seemed to be possible. Reform movements, even sects, were composed of people who missed something in the church, left and went ahead with their own understanding, born out of the reaction against the group they came from. In one or two generations the outside enemy against whom they rebelled already became faceless; and later on you find a religion only based on the originally emphasized truth, leaving out everything else, 'taking apart the whole, and concentrating just on one part of it to the exclusion of the rest'.

Some Baptists, on the contrary, will tell you that they never saw themselves as a separate Church, but as a movement that existed from the very beginning, contemporaneously with the first believers. Adult baptism, free acceptance of grace, individual conversion have always been around. Later this movement was submerged, overlaid with official Christianity that took a different direction with the Councils and with Constantine. Throughout history this movement emerged again, in the late Middle Ages, with the Hussites, the Waldensians and many other reform movements without name or fame, then spectacularly with the Anabaptists, then later on in England and America in industrial times. Are they more numerous today than before? Perhaps they have increased in numbers. But maybe the others just paid less attention to them before. They were there all the time, in large numbers, linked to the whole American experience. My friend's hunch is that there is no big change in numbers, but that they got richer, can afford a lot more, living in that part of the country that is now wealthy and booming, while it used to be considered as poor and somewhat oppressed. There is some irony in the fact that they have now surfaced as the dominant religious force in that part of the country, while traditionally the Baptist movement was always over against the society in power, always a social protest movement, representing an intense, personal, radical, individualistic conversion-type of religion among the poor.

I tell my friend that in my opinion all movements in Christianity, after thorough analysis, can be seen as emerging from one central, often mystical intuition about the immense horizon of God. Such an analysis can of course lead to a reduction of the message they convey, but it can also clarify the basic thrust that underlines the whole branched-out, built-up structure. The reality they speak about is so great and vast that thinkers, even the most comprehensive ones among them, could not grasp the whole horizon, but absolutized the importance of the few lights they were capable of discerning. If this is true, if Luther or Wesley or even St Augustine worked out of one fundamental insight, then it is possible to see them as complementary, as multi-faceted approaches to the same mystery. Luther, St Ignatius of Loyola, St Teresa of Avila – all living at the same time – should be studied structurally: what do they have in common in their speaking about God? What are their basic, mystical intuitions? If you take away the polemical aspects of their doctrines, caused by the political, social, cultural context and the theological confrontations of the sixteenth century, would you not discover approaches that are not merely compatible, but complementary, different but pointing along different lines to the same uniqueness of God?

We would then have to search for the basic gifts in others' beliefs and churches, to discern their specific contribution to the total understanding, learn from the others and reconcile in ourselves all these manifold expressions of the human response to God's message. And the central question would then be: how do you forge in yourself a real communion underneath all the diversity, embracing the diversity too? The individual experience would be one way to be penetrated by the mystery of the Resurrection, the monastic experience could be another and so forth, because communion does not mean agreeing with one another, negotiating compromises or deciding to act in the same way, but accepting a common belonging, a first communion, a sense of being bonded to the others who are as important to my salvation as my own personal answer may be to myself or to them. All the individual selves would not be complete until we connect them with all the others in the one mystical body of Christ, according to the Pauline image.

Most people would say: you are the way you are, you believe I'm the way I am, leave me alone and I will leave you alone. This tolerance is better than attacking or imprisoning each another, but it is not good enough. We belong together. Is agreement the next step after tolerance? No, differences are not in themselves destructive; there is an understanding of common life which is nourished by differences. When I meet people who are different, the aim is not that they change or that they change me, but that they become more themselves in the communion we are trying to express together. It may be that we cannot think and perceive in the same way, because the reality that we are thinking about is so vast, but we can sense that there is a common reality. 'In Him we live and have our being.' This reality truly transcends us, and yet we are immersed in it. It is at the same time in ourselves and part of something not ourselves. This communion which we can live out together will not solve our disagreements, will not teach us what to do practically – for instance what stand to take concerning atomic weapons. Everything will still have to be worked out. But a deep image of who you are, that we are linked together, will emerge underneath our differences.

My friend sums up this idea by saying: 'Your real self includes the other; that is the mystical body of Christ. Probably we should go around for a while saying that: you don't have an individual self, there is one self, Christ, which is more close to the truth than extreme individualism.'

Is this individualism found only in Evangelical Christianity? Do Catholics and Episcopalians emphasize another image, the sense of common belonging? Perhaps in their external forms. But if ordinary Catholics and Baptists would meet – unfortunately they don't – they would probably feel the same way about themselves and God. They all reflect the individualism of American culture, and to that extent the rituals that suggest another approach are perhaps only simply an overlay. Do they represent the American experience? The Catholics, at least until recently, were dependent on Europe for their vision of life; the immigrants brought their particular interpretations of life reflecting European culture into the American 'immigrant church'; Catholic priests were often trained in Europe; the artistic life, the cultural expressions, the hymns, even the language were all European. America did not inherit society; apart from destroying native American societies, they created a new one. Grown-ups created society; they didn't inherit it from their parents. Americans helped to create a common life; there was not a common life already existing within which people became individuals.

Now I understand why the Baptist minister seemed so evasive when I asked him how people could become ambassadors of reconciliation in the midst of the inequalities and separations between the white, Mexican-American and black neighbourhoods of San Antonio. Basically he was saying: be reconciled within yourself first, and then you can choose to share that reconciliation with other people. First of all you are who you are within yourself. Belonging doesn't come first. The 'fellowship' is not a reality greater than the individuals that make it up. What counts is the encounter between the individual and God. Even baptism is an external symbol for what has occurred between the individual and God, and that can only happen by the free choice of individuals. Even if Baptists would say 'once you accept your Saviour, you are no longer an individual or on your own', I think they would insist that the one self includes only those who accept the Saviour in the same way.

But to get a glimpse, to experience something of the mystical body of Christ, we have to let all the others into our existence, not only our immediate neighbours but people throughout the world. Societies and individuals, collectively and individually, we all live like people cut off from the other half of ourselves; we lack that other part of ourselves, even if we never acknowledge this. There is a separation between those people and institutions which have a monopoly on the power and on the word and those people who are kept in servitude and are without a voice, but who often, be it in silence, are bearers of that life which the others are losing. Half of our sight, half of our hearing, half of our sensitivity is missing, because we have preferred to cut ourselves off from that other half which seemed useless or unimportant. And so we suffer, because we are not able to build up our lives, our worlds, together. To aspire to live out a communion with all people is not a luxury, one more outreach to be undertaken, it is a vital necessity as soon as we discover that the life of the others who had rejected us or whom we have denied is absent from our own life. Through the Resurrection, a new reality has made its way into humanity's depths, into me – yes – but also into the whole universe, into the world, into history; the Risen Lord leads humanity to a final fulfilment, integrating all that has fallen apart, all that was lost. It is happening now, independently of us, independently of our 'yes' and 'amen'. But we have the privilege of having been chosen to know this deepest secret of history, not in order to feel more safe or more 'saved' than the others, but as a gift to share and to let shine in the world. We can do this, not necessarily by multiplying our activities, but by the action of faith – we are people invited to bear in themselves the secret of communion which the Risen Lord is establishing among us, as He prepares the Kingdom, until 'all our being will be clothed by Him'.

Searching for roots in California
Ministers of different denominations with whom I'm sitting together for a quiet conversation tell me that the life of the people in the Bay Area is overwhelmingly superficial. The individual homes, the wealth and the rest of it I caught a glimpse of this morning, driving around in the rich areas of the Mid-peninsula, is all only developing life at the surface level. 'Surface equals dead. You know what an antonym for depth is: heartless. We're in an extraordinarily heartless time of human living. With no imagination.' Generations of people are estranged from one another, estranged from themselves. People don't really know themselves. They are constantly entertained by the media. If I can stay on the surface, perhaps I can avoid pain. Significance, ultimacy, depth – it is all gone. One of the first things that begins to develop as one goes inside, dealing with the real images of

life – the imaginative life – is eaten up by the flashy attacks on the screen of the videogames. 'We are not just talking about one neighbourhood, we're talking about twenty-four, twenty-five million people in California, the size of many nations on earth.' 'Is it different in Holland?'

I was just thinking how often I noticed the severity of Americans when they talk about themselves. Is this an expression of compensation for the inability to stop or to change disquieting evolutions in a huge country? In a small country you are immediately invited on a TV show if you have the least thing to say, and you can address the whole country, call upon your compatriots if you want to lose your anonymity, and eventually influence the Government. That's how the peace movement of the Dutch churches became such a success. You can do something which is not condemned in advance to uselessness. In a large country a lot of patience, perseverance or heroism is needed if you want to change anything. How to get this across? Is it different in Holland? you asked. No, but people there talk to one another. You sit on the train, the man next to you will offer you a cigar and you will have a conversation about politics, life, death and religion the one- or two-hour ride that takes you out of the country. People don't keep away from one another. They still have a feeling of belonging together, because the space which they inhabit is so limited that you have to deal with the phenomenon of all those other people you see all the time. Moreover, Calvinism has instilled an irresistible love for confrontation; fighting supposes a certain understanding of belonging together. There is still an energy, not undermined by consumerism and laid-back indifference that pushes people to do some- thing if things don't please them or if 'principles' are in danger, which is another Calvinistic archetype. Is is accu- rate that I hear among Americans more of the echo of helplessness, a complaint at being unable to cope with the complexity of problems? Do they therefore turn the ac- cumulated aggressiveness against themselves, depicting

131

apocalyptic scenes of America's destiny and creating a confused vulnerability?

Of course, in the unspoken part of the lives of many people in California, the rootlessness must be a factor. Most people come here from somewhere else, from the East or from the West, and there is not a lot of tradition around. Elsewhere, in the Midwest or on the East Coast, things are settled, rooted in tradition and it's hard to change. Freedom is a blessing, but the other side of the coin is the insecurity that rootlessness creates. Has there not been in America for a long time a naive optimism that difficulties of any sort could be overcome? A kind of blind, stubborn faith in progress, sustained by the seemingly never ending upsurge of the economy? An ignorance of the limits of the possible, a result of the frontier ideology? It seems to me that today all over America, in conversations, on the faces of the people and even in the media some wrinkles are becoming visible, some rumbling is becoming audible. The squeeze of the economic policies, the fattening of the military establish-ment, the decadence of America's radiance in the other parts of the world – in the fifties Americans were reputedly believed to keep young, enthusiastic eyes even in old age – are hastening the feelings of insecurity and uncertainty. People are getting worried. Things are beginning to shake in the vaults of people's minds. Whether they acknowledge it or not, below the surface something like an earthquake is beginning to make its presence felt. Is it different in other countries of the Northern hemisphere? they asked. No, I say, but there there is no California where people swarm as to an archetypal place, like queen bees who want to change. Does the mystique of the place not have some influence, more or less consciously felt, on the people's reaction to this uncertainty? We always hear that people in California are exposed to just about every conceivable spiritual pursuit, from Tibetan masters to gurus, from esoteric Christian cults to sufism. Is there in this great cultural basin, centre of universal learning, with Stanford around the corner, in this

132

hub of intercultural mixing no creative response that descends from the slopes of all this industrious contemplation?

I also say to myself that if ministers speak to you in a depressed way about the general trends of our civilization, it means that they are busy redefining the vocation of the Church. Where there is a need, especially a need for spiritual grounding, the Church should answer. It is worthwhile for the Church to listen intensely to the signs of the times, if it leads her to adapt herself so as to touch people in their depths and to awaken there that lost paradise which is the garden where we walk with God. How capable is the Church in the Bay Area of bringing about that spiritual grounding, after the activist sixties and the drifting seventies?

First voice: there is an agony in the Church going on today. There is an agony for me in just being the pastor of a church. I claim that the Church's heritage is to be a power, a force for reconciliation in the world. And seeing it's so far from that, I'm suffering. There are in the world signs of a springtime of the Church, and my temptation would be to leave here and to go wherever there is a sign of hope, to be part of that and thus, ultimately, fulfil my own life. And that God won't let me do that yet. He hasn't opened that door. I see my vocation right now as being called to suffer with Christ in His agony, to suffer from the Church.

Second voice: we don't have many symbols, symbolic places, holy places. We desecrated those in mainline Western Christianity. We need places of silence, like a little bit of land set aside for the distinct purpose of encountering God. There is an overwhelming need for this in the life of Christians and other people in California. There are pilgrimages lost in our world, the idea of going somewhere to search for God should be reawakened. There is a need for pilgrimage in the human heart. Those kinds of holy activities have been exorcized, even among Catholics but most of all in the Protestant world. Only now is it coming back – liturgy, silence, spiritual direction, pilgrimage, colours, images, candles, icons, spirituality, litanies, incense, meditation and contemplation. The world's centre for microdata industry where they make the tiny little silicon chips that are changing the face of our information gathering, in the Silicon Valley, is right down here. Fifteen minutes away. In a world in which the advanced technology industry has come to dominate, there is at the same time a rising interest in silence, iconography, chanting. People are yearning for sounds, not the sounds of the micro-processors, but perhaps for that primordial sound that must have come from the great abyss that made us all. People want to be touched in the depths as well as to flash little letters on the screen. The Church's ministry is to remind people of the other side. Jesus went to the other side.

Third voice: our Church has been primarily activist and intellectual. Our denomination is burning up from the inside, from the leadership on down. Church growth, fast expansion is the big thing, as we have, for various reasons, lost many members over the past years. What fundamentally has weakened the Church has been its insensitivity, not to the world's needs but to the voice of God. A lot of money is pumped into mission programmes and local programmes as well, in order to reach out into the community, to bring in the lonely people, to combat racism and militarism, to be in dialogue with different professional milieux. We have been very sensitive to the world in our mission activity, but insensitive to the forming of a vision within us, a vision to remould society, a new vision replacing the old ones that are no longer adequate to the needs of the vast, rapid social changes and personal human changes we're going through in this day and age. The institution is wandering, does not know where to lead to, it has no dominant call, is very busy on raising money and on programmes. I wish I could say there is hope, you know.

We are getting into a passionate discussion about ways in which this imbalance in the Church between vision and

134

action, rootedness in the peace of God and concern about the warmongers of the world should be redressed. For a while now I've been worried that the search for a closer awareness of God is more and more separated from the 'institution' of the Church. One minister quotes a French Protestant theologian who affirms that God has turned his back on the institutional Church. I feel a kind of instinctive reaction against this way of dividing the Church up in bits and pieces, one piece being the dimension baptized 'institution', one other piece being my personal ecclesial belonging. The institution seems to be seen as a sort of objective block of Christianity far outside of the walls of my subjective authenticity. I don't believe in the perseverance of individuals without the framework of the Church, unless we are all to become heroes. Separating the institution from ourselves and from the range of our own responsibility is somehow repeating the old Protestant impoverishing rupture that took place at the Reformation and that has got wider and wider since then. The institution is not only that bundle of mailing lists that glides out of the computer or the self-sufficient structure that would even keep on turning long after all the Christians have left the churches. The institution is the link with former generations of Christians and with Christians all over the world today. The institution is us, in a corporate sense. Furthermore, very simply, take a walk from time to time through the corridors of your institution, you'll meet a lot of spiritual people who are asking themselves questions like: how can we find the inspiration for our work in prayer? How should we become more present, by visits and personal sharing, to what is happening on a neighbourhood level? Speaking about the institution as the source of all evil is already isolating myself outside of it as well as making out of it a thing that leads its own life. We need the institution, as we need a building for worship, a Bible to be read, the Eucharist for communion, a body to go to church. And if we call the central administration an institution, is the parish or congregation or retreat-house or family not an institution? How can one imagine the continuity of believers meeting together in the future – people who don't select one another because of the same age or the same opinions on a social and political level or the same opposition against the institution ... – if not with the help of an institution that is called the parish or congregation or Christian community? What about the poor, or those who would never ring the doorbell of a private home but sometimes push the door of a parish church?

But finally we get this theme out of our way, because we make a difference between the professed goals of the institution with the people in it and the unlucky experiences that sometimes people can have. Ministers suffer more from it than lay people; they are closer. They don't always see a spiritual vision behind a bureaucratic institution run by management styles rather than by pastoral care. It hurts them too, because the institution with its visibility determines the way the Church, and ultimately the Gospel, is seen by the people. And they say that right here in the Bay Area they suffer from an excessive institutionalization on the side of the Church as well as from a life of superficiality among the people. They would like to see the whole Church adopt the priority of spiritual grounding, of discovery of one's depths, of empowerment, of silence that harbours the presence of Christ.

The second point I try to make is that in my opinion the temptation of individualism, the anti-institutional attitude and the distorted balance between spiritual life and intervention in society should be countered by a greater openness towards the Catholic and Eastern-Orthodox traditions. It is only through reconciliation with them that a way out of the existing dilemmas can be found, in the wider communion of the whole Church. Protestant traditions have in most cases carried to the extreme all the consequences of separation, down to individualism and conformity to the contemporary world, so much that the vision of the

136

communion of the Church has often got lost. We seem to have reached a point of no return. It is no solution to withdraw even further in a last purist effort. It is time to knit together the threads of the robe of Christ and to rediscover the whole Christian tradition with all its components.

On this question of the vocation of the Church we are not yet on the same wavelength. One minister who leads a retreat centre tries to explain to me that their engagement with the world is disengagement. They 'exaggerate' their task, he admits, in a hyperbolic way. Christian institutions are too quick, too rushed to solutions. What happens to contemporary ministry in a media-oriented, in a quick transfer of information society is that any new system that comes along is immediately adopted, 'gobbled up', he says, baptized and then sent into the churches, things like transactional analysis which has been sweeping California to various systems of psychology or management techniques. This expresses such an engagement with the surrounding culture in the sense of imitation and such an adaptation to the insights and methods the culture has to offer that the vision of how this culture can be opened to the Kingdom of God is lost. Therefore withdrawal is right now what is needed for refashioning our own vision and methods and strategies. Of course, withdrawal is a practical problem; the whole Church can't move into the desert. Should there however not be at the core of every parish, synod or region a community of disengagement, of withdrawal? The task of these communities would be to engage the culture according to the voice of the Spirit rather than from whatever society is telling us.

I can certainly understand that Christians are called to withdraw from time to time from daily existence, to leave everything, to search for God in the desert. But can I preach that as a vocation for the Church, and indeed base a retreat-house or a place of withdrawal on that assumption, or presumption? It seems to me too that disengagement and withdrawal are negative terms. There is nothing in it that can take hold of my imagination. At Taizé I wouldn't be able to speak to young people counselling them to withdraw, and – perhaps curiously as a monk – I don't have the feeling of having withdrawn; on the contrary, I feel myself at the heart of the Church.

This may be true for people who come to Taizé, is the answer. In the Bay Area – and that's what you were asking about – withdrawal *is* negative and it is needed. Americans have prided themselves on their industry, adaptation and inquisitiveness, but now that part of American culture is gone, we have exhausted ourselves. We have applied the same things in terms of religion. The last thing our Church needs to do is to make any more social pronouncements until it knows where they really come from. They should tremble or weep about those situations rather than send declarations out through the media. An easy pronouncement and we go on to the next item of business. There is no silence in the assemblies.

But we all agree in saying that Christians are called to live in depth. One needs therefore silence and self-confrontation, although I would prefer words like deep listening, surrender, rebirth. I tell about that person who seemed disillusioned about the fact that in our society nothing of value is left any more, no God, no State, no Church, the only thing left is the discovery of one's self. Is California not known, perhaps only mythologically, as the land of self-discovery? Is the search for the self – and the discovery of God along the way – not ambiguous, at least as a term? Does it not sound selfish, should not silence for the Christian be a way of being with Christ, with the other, not with ourselves?

The answer is that silence should not lead to individualism but to 'a very deep awareness of the gift of the human person, of the riches within both the light and the dark within us'. The self-discovery of the 'me'-generation is narcissistic, 'self-serving', while for the Christian it becomes

138

a means of ministry and the discovery of communion with other people. 'I can only find communion with you if I can find communion with myself, because I can't give you the attention you deserve as a child of God, if I'm not aware of the attending to my own self and to God who resides within me, of whom I'm unaware much of the time, till I become aware of the deeper dimensions of myself.'

Twentieth-century religion in New Orleans

For several days now I've been ruminating the same questions, on my daily walk from St Augustine's to St Jude's (the saint of impossible causes) on Rampart Street. I have been interested to plunge into the depth of the island's religious history, but I am equally interested in knowing what image of the *future* of religion can be found here. Perhaps it is easier to get some vision in an historical city with its deep strata of centuries' worth of religious experiences than in other American settings where the denominational experiences are laid out parallel to each other and in simple juxtaposition. Are there some ideas around of a future towards which the dried-up bones of the past, if only they could be brought to life again, should march? Suppose a spiritual tornado swept away the levee ridges that keep fiercely independent Christian traditions impervious to one another – what would then be the cornerstones, the basic structures that would have to be saved at all costs, on the day we would find the courage to wrap up together again all the spread-out religious bits and pieces into the unique communion the Church was meant to be?

I push the revolving door of the TV station on Rampart Street (WWLTV, channel 14), so discreetly designed that I had at first completely overlooked the building, though it stands exactly between St Jude's and St Augustine's. The station is owned by the Jesuits, or more precisely by Xavier University. After the radio came under government control in 1930, regulations for radio licences were tightened and many private organizations (one-half of the radio licences had previously been owned by churches and schools) had to stop their wireless experience. The Jesuits 'happened', as they say, to stay in the business more or less by 'inertia' (they own two other radio stations in Lafayette, La.). The result is that they now have to cope as a religious order with a flourishing, fully commercialized station that certainly produces at least some scholarships for poor students at the university!

The first thing I see, as I enter the large study of the Jesuit who is the liaison person between the university and the station is the high stack of books on his desk, written by and about ... Luther. Luther in a TV station? In New Orleans? That's the last place I expected to find this figure of the late European Middle Ages! I hardly have time to mumble my questions, the Jesuit has already intercepted my glance at the pile of books and starts to talk about Luther. Periodically in the course of our conversation, the Jesuit bursts out in a loud, marvellous peal of laughter which translates his happiness about an association of ideas or indicates his uneasiness with an all-too-audacious statement. In those intervals I try from time to time to reformulate my initial questions, until I discover that my teacher has perfectly understood my concern, almost before I entered the room and that I simply have to wait until the class is over.... If I give him the opportunity to unwind the thread of his vision, I will understand that Luther was necessary in order to come up with an answer to my question.

He is standing next to his desk in this air-conditioned room with Luther's 'Table Talk' in his hand. And I remember standing only a few months ago in the very room in Wittenberg in Eastern Germany where Luther talked at the table. Martin Luther is contemplating his baby, Martin Junior, nursing and says: 'See that child nursing. Child, your enemies are the Pope, the bishops, Duke George, Ferdinand and the devil and there you are, sucking unconcernedly.' Even at a moment like this he remembers

140

who he is against. I'm remembering that sometimes I had to choose spiritual readings for compline and that, glancing through Luther's works for some fresh insights for today, I had to clear my way through the invectives and injuries, and to cut out here and there a part of a sentence to make up a spiritual text. Luther was a man of opposition, he needed the dialectical element. Why is the 'Catechism' so important in Luther's heritage? Because in a catechism it is possible to prove how one is different from everyone else. In his preaching and so much of his writing Luther teaches a dialectical religion. Of course there are other aspects in his work, especially the emphasis on music, where you can't be dialectical. Music is beyond tensions. You can't have a hymn *against* something, music brings together. Luther would take hymns from anywhere and write beautiful tributes to music in prefaces to a book of polyphonies which had a Catholic origin. There he was ecumenical.

In reality, the dialectical element in faith and theology can be found not only in Luther, but in everything that came thereafter, as long as the print medium dominated the communication processes. The print medium made it possible to express differences. Catechisms, proving that we are not Seventh Day Adventists, not Jehovah's Witnesses, not Episcopalians, that we are Catholics, were printed. But now we have religion on television, where it is impossible to make credal differentiation. You cannot say like in a book, 'We believe this contrary to ABCDEFG. You have to present the image of a loving person. You can't speak about God as a loving Father, if you don't show a picture of a kind person with a child. People have to be trained, because at first they are uneasy with the fact that on television you cannot distinguish yourself from the other groups.'

The Jesuit goes on Sundays to the prison, to the women one week and the men the next week (the Protestants do the opposite). The thing that amazes him with the mostly black prisoners who are illiterate is that they have some kind of a basic religious structure, rooted in their lives, which is singing hymns. Religious culture is transmitted by songs, especially among the blacks (the majority of people in New Orleans proper are blacks). 'Black people have that beautiful folk religion.' There is, in other words, no dialectical religion. They very rarely make a credal differentiation. They talk about the basics: God loves you, you are a sinner and you can be saved, it is a message of hope. These people, who are the lowest class of society, know all the stories – they know about the plagues of Egypt, they know about the crossing of the Red Sea, it is very easy to talk about Easter to them. These are people who are very ignorant, but when they sing a song they can sing sixteen verses – they know them all. If you would ask them: How many sacraments are there? How many books are there in the Bible? or the question in the catechism: Who is God?, they could hardly put together a sentence or they wouldn't know. If you say, 'Today, our reading is from St Luke', they would have a hard time finding St Luke in the Bible and you would see them going with their fingers through their Bibles up and down, unfamiliar with this kind of culture. But they are very familiar with the faith that is transmitted in song; they have never known any other religion. They have never gone to a Bible class. Is this linked to the experience of oppression? It is linked to preliteracy. For most Churches you have to be able to read. The legacy of the Reformation, Protestant and Catholic, is print-orientated culture. It becomes middle-class religion. Up until the fifteenth century no one knew how many sacraments there were and they still went to heaven. In the sixteenth century you get in church the phenomenon of the preacher who has the main role in his classroom filled with pews. In popular religion, especially in black religion, the preacher never has it to himself, he dialogues, the audience participates, the audience is never passive.

The Jesuit goes once a month to preach at St Francis de Sales', where they have incorporated the black culture into the worship (at Corpus Christi on St Bernard Avenue where educated blacks go there is no participatory singing). The people talk all the time. They tell you what they don't like about it. It is the worst sign if they are silent. In a white church, silence is the best. In a black church, people have to react. Sometimes they sing. Another thing about that kind of participatory service is that people love to be in church. Church is a play for them. Other people would say, 'Well, I can go to this church and I'll be back in one hour'. In prison priests are allowed to stay only one hour. The most frequent complaint is that the service is not long enough. It is not because the preacher is so great, but because they are interested. They have a tremendous religious culture and they know, from within, that Jesus loves them. They aren't sure what he demands of them. They very rarely talk about morality. They're not very good on the ten commandments, but they're very good on the notion of salvation that Jesus frees them and that there is hope.

Vice versa, going to the prison has given to this Jesuit great hope. Pastors and ministers normally expect precise knowledge. They say, 'My people know absolutely nothing. They don't know the story of Christ, they don't know the prophecies, they don't know the book of Genesis, they don't know where we stand on justification by faith alone, they have no appreciation of the liturgy.' Because they think of the church as a school, the people never know enough. Anyhow, you can never know all there is to know about the Bible and theology. Often there is the feeling that you should not preach about the Word of God until you know everything. The Jesuit, who has a doctor's degree, who has written books and was teaching at a university and can't therefore be accused of anti-intellectualism, is saying that the amount of knowledge that it takes to save your soul is vastly exaggerated. 'What impresses me the most is how little you need to know in order to love God, how these people in prison, these people in the lowest strata of society have a firm grasp that there is hope for them, that God has saved them and that God has redeemed them from their sins, even if they don't have a firm grasp on what God wants from them.'

Folk religion nourishes itself by songs, music and all kinds of symbols. And the symbolic elements in religion are ecumenical, more so than the intellectual ones that are dialectical. The rituals of burial are very elaborate in New Orleans. The Jesuit will be going in a little while to the funeral of a two-week-old baby, the son of one of the ladies who works for the TV station. He goes to at least two funerals a week. The black funeral is very elaborate. The body is taken to the church and people call from when they get off work until about 9pm. Then, at 9, the service begins. The black service is always at night. It lasts about three hours. The next morning only a few people accompany the body to the grave. The service is more singing than preaching. We need rituals. Some people say that God despises all these rituals and externals and that religion must be a religion of the heart. But the Jesuit thinks that, although our religion will never be pure before the sight of the Lord, God loves all these rituals. There are not enough rituals in Catholicism today. It is too intellectual, rigid, automatic. The reason, he thinks, is the fact that Catholics have moved up the social ladder, become 'bourgeoisified' and therefore there is no folk religion any more. He speaks about those priests who get up and talk about Karl Rahner's most recent book, and he thinks that people are not interested in that. This is, incidentally, one of the re-proaches made by black people in the Catholic church: when a white preacher comes, he talks about politics; when a black preacher comes, he talks about God. The white preacher brings the middle-class concerns – economics, women's rights, the freeze, unemployment. But for them, poverty is not new, they have always been unemployed and for them all Presidents were bad. The lower class needs more immediate gratification. They need more the vision of God as hope. It has to touch them closer at hand. They are concerned about their family and their immediate surround-

144

ings. They want their children to be educated, but they don't think about fancy schools, they think in terms of moral education. The big difficulty they have with schools is that the schools do not make the children behave. Lower-class people, both black and white, find it hard to talk in abstractions about poverty and peace. It is the more immediate family that touches them. 'You can talk to prisoners about death – they will all be dry-eyed; you talk to them about drunkenness, they will be dry-eyed; but if you talk to them about how they neglect their children, they will all cry.'

Young people love ritual. They have the ritual of courtship, the ritual of their own music, the huge ritual of sports. They insist on everything being done exactly as it has always been done. 'We try to bring young people to church, so we say, we'll cut out all the ritual, and then we wonder why they don't come. The Taizé Pilgrimage is a beautiful ritual.' The Jesuit's father, who never went to communion on Sunday, always went on first Friday, according to the recommendation in St Marguerite-Mary Alacocque's vision in Paray-le-Monial of the Sacred Heart: 'Those who receive communion during the first Friday of the month nine successive times will die in my friendship'. The Jesuit's father finally decided, fifteen years before he died, that he should go to communion. Up until that time he would not go to communion on Christmas, but he went on every first Friday. Superstitious? It spoke to the ordinary people. New Orleans is a good town for ritual: they have the ritual jazz funeral for people who die, the ritual Mardi Gras parade, they have the traditional King party at the feast of Epiphany. On that day the King cake is served and inside the cake is a plastic figure of the child Jesus. You cut the cake and the person who gets the baby has to give a party. Therefore New Orleans is a kind of religious place. People become converts to religion and adopt the ritual that preserves folk beliefs better than books. At the TV station there are executives who make huge salaries and who still go to St Jude's for novenas. Where else in America do you still find novenas? New Orleans is one of the few places where you can find a black Protestant church dedicated to a saint. They love the saints.

It is not surprising to me that the Jesuit feels perfectly at ease at a Charismatic meeting or at the Assembly of God. The singing, the participation, the emotions, the more juicy, more personal and popular religion has enormous potential, in the Jesuit's eyes. It is the most ecumenical movement in New Orleans, he says. 'What do you say when you go to a Charismatic group? Praise you, Jesus, praise you, Lord! Thank you! A Protestant and a Catholic can say the same thing. You don't say "Thank you through St Jude" or "Thank you that I'm saved by grace alone and not by works", you just say "Thank you, Jesus".'

Twentieth-century religion seen from the perspective of New Orleans 'Mediterranean' Catholicism? A folk religion, a popular religion, a ritualistic religion, a symbolic religion, an ecumenical religion.

The Jesuit has to leave for the funeral. In the elevator he is still completing his improvisation on twentieth-century religion. He says that the bishop was asking him, 'How are we going to tell the people how many sacraments we have?' But he thinks that the people ask, 'Can you give me the right answer, the good news?' and that we shouldn't tell bad news (like 'you can't fornicate'!) of morals and dogma, but the joyful news that God loves you, God forgives you. And then it is time for a thunderous peal of laughter, right at the revolving door.

On Rampart Street, in the sun, walking back, I remember walking as a child next to my father on the Kruislaan in Amsterdam. At that time we were Calvinists from top to toe. To the left the baseball team (I admired above all the pitcher) was playing. But for me it was forbidden to look in that direction. Sunday was a holy day without ice-cream, without restaurants and trolleys, without playing cards in the house or soccer outside with the kids in the street, because it was considered wrong to amuse yourself on the day of the Lord and – social criticism – to oblige the trolley conductor to work on Sunday. I have never criticized my father for that (later on we spent long Sundays together looking at the sports news on TV), because there was so much worthwhile in this 'inner-worldly asceticism', as Troeltsch called it, and I don't at all regret the Sunday afternoons of my youth sticking pictures of whatever references I could find about Egyptian mythology into a thick black stitched book. And I was happy singing hymns and listening, sometimes sitting on the steps of the high pulpit facing the thousands of people who, like me, came three times on Sundays to church to learn and to be uplifted.

But I understand that we all need, in this age, the experience of all the expressions of Church life, beyond the antagonistic attitudes, left-overs from the past. We need a rebirth together in order to hear the Master say today: 'I will give them a feast and will serve them' and, in the words of St Ignatius, the patron of my Jesuit friend, to talk to Him as a friend to a friend.

An Armful of Gifts — New Ministries

Nusquama's Interchurch Centre

Nusquama sounds American-Indian. Thinking about that name I wonder if I have invented that city or not; the atlas I consulted doesn't mention any Nusquama. The other cities of this book are immediately recognizable on the outside circle of the American rainbow. I suppose Nusquama must be somewhere in mid-air between Montana and Oklahoma. Isn't it logical to include a less known city from the heart of America to complete the total picture? In a letter to Erasmus (3 September 1517) Thomas More calls his island Utopia 'Nusquama' (from the Latin word 'nusquam', 'nowhere'). So More at least knew about its existence. Intrigued, I decided to visit the place and to share the life of the Church there (in the local vocabulary the plural doesn't exist any more). It was a very stimulating experience, although I was surprised to find so many things similar to the best initiatives I had found in the other cities. Sometimes I saw no difference at all. Most often the inhabitants of Nusquama seemed like people everywhere else; some consequences however became more explicit, as if in other places everything is present – gifts, initiatives, new dynamism and openness – but without that final step which makes the Church a sign of contradiction, a place very different from the surrounding society and as a matter of fact an anticipation of what many who struggle in society hope for. And that is the way the Church in Nusquama has become a hearth, a source, a warm light in that city and beyond.

All the people I met on the first day of my stay in Nusquama were talking about the changes in the Interchurch centre. Suppose such a change were made in New

York, where a similar centre stands on Riverside Drive. Nobody would believe it. It is hard to become a sign of transparency behind the walls of a centre built to last for centuries like an impregnable fortress on top of the Alps. A church building that looks exactly like the RCA or the Chrysler buildings acquires a built-in stamp of eternity. In Nusquama the inner conflict people felt about the incongruities of the Interchurch centre on which for fifty years an average of six floors a year were added each time a new denomination had started, had finally been resolved in a revolutionary set of decisions that seemed the only way left to make a difference that would really be felt. The board of directors, in an historic session, aided by the despair of architects whose technical discussions to build towers on towers on towers had ended in Babylonian confusion, had decided to stop this visible expression of the Church's disunity. While they had put up passively for so long with what they had called 'the ecclesial creativity' in Nusquama, they now recognized that another strategy had to replace this centrifugal proliferation as reflected in the hundreds of yellow pages in the telephone directory under the heading 'Church'. There had even been some doubts if this heading was still justified because of its vagueness, unreality and archeological resonance. A large consultation had expressed the general uneasiness. One of the directors had spoken at the session about the necessity of 'crawling back to the essential waters'.

Practically speaking, this meant two things. First, the priority in the coming years would be to instill in the life of the denominations a dynamic of unity instead of division, to witness to the same creativity as before but in reversing the objective. They would no longer add other floors. This seemed to them the most important decision within their reach to express their refusal of further divisions. But secondly, they announced that at each step taken by the denominations in the direction of mutual recognition and unity they would empty the floor used by the one of the

149

two denominations that had ceased to exist in its old form. Essential data would be thrown into the computer. Paper was recycled and sold to the Hallmark company so that they could print thank-you-for-being-part-of-the-one-holy-catholic-church cards. The empty floor would then be refurnished as a shelter for transients who are numerous in Nusquama during the months they migrate from the cold Midwest to California or the Southwest. The personnel who had worked on that floor and who couldn't be simply sent away were offered a job with the homeless as a work of hospitality, paid for by the two churches that had redis-covered their unity as a penance and also as a first common effort. It seemed important to the directors to offer not only a place and the nice view over the prairies but to make out of the available space – along the lines of their emphasis on creativity – a home. In the future other floors could be attributed to a housing association for the elderly, a hospital for chronic diseases, life communities for handicapped and non-handicapped, emergency housing for runaways and so forth, with the explicit aim of breaking down separations between all those categories of people, and to allow an intermingling of generations and classes by which they hoped to give another sign of unity. Some of the directors had volunteered to move in with their family. For the time being the other floors could continue to function but each floor received a deadline by when it would have to make itself superfluous. It was made clear that they should not move out to somewhere else in the suburbs but operate from now on in such a way that simplification would occur gradually until they finally reached the unity with the church on the next floor.

People in Nusquama emphasized the fact that all this was not the result of a bureaucratic decision but the fruit of a sudden deeply spiritual intuition that had overpowered the leadership of the churches, starting with those who had always been considered the most reluctant to agree to any change. Commentators expressed their admiration for the

150

sincerity of the board of directors in implementing – after having used that word for years and years *ad nauseam*, now they *did* it – and influencing a movement of adaptation which would make the witness of the Church more authentic and up-to-date. They also applauded a fundamental rediscovery of the interdependent ecumenical and social vocations of the Church.

Forms of suburban-urban solidarity
A restaurant owner is at the origin of a widespread effort of suburban-urban solidarity in Nusquama. Because of his readings about Haiti and other underdeveloped countries he had started to think about how food could be channelled to places like that. Discussing this with his staff he had come to the conclusion that it was preferable to calculate on every meal sold in one of his restaurants a certain percentage (ten per cent) and to send that money to Haiti or other countries so that people can eat. After having done this for several years he became interested in the urban areas in which people need food. A lot of consultation took place. One of the results was the decision of suburban and urban churches to start a process of sharing everything together over a period of seven years, progressively extended and intensified. It is not only a question of pooling money. Two churches – one in the city and one in the suburbs – become really one and are invited to mix in the choirs, the parish council, the ladies' club, and so forth: there is this continual interaction. Every week a delegation goes to the other church, and parish members rotate. They meet for worship, meals and discussions around tables in the basement to list all the needs and to cope with the problem of inequality on all levels. It involves questions about the school system, the differences in tuition at the private colleges, the number of cars people have, the living conditions, vacation places, problems of stress and depression, drug problems – all on the basis of the perspective of the community of goods as described in the Book of Acts. It is not an easy process and a

lot of aggression has emerged. But the parish council keeps insisting that this search for sharing in the precise details of our lives has to be pursued with perseverance if we want to have the right to come up with a more just vision of society as a whole.

In one low-income area where block associations were doubled by 'better' block associations because of a conflict about ways to fight crime on the block and to determine how much money had to be allocated to a local garden for senior citizens, a church, working through the community organization, has been able to organize shadow block associations for reconciliation. The members don't leave the other groups but try to act for peace in the midst of worsening divisions and conflicts. For instance, they invite for dinner the officers of two block associations that are fighting each another, trying to find ways for collaboration to become possible once again. In this area the question had come up whether an apartment owned by a co-op could be sold by the tenant for a much higher price to somebody who had not been accepted by the other tenants. People were divided about this question of resale policy. To prevent a split, a certain number of people on the block wrote a letter from which I would like to quote some parts: 'Our needs differ. The amount of time, work, money, commitment we each have put in our apartments, into maintaining, renovating the building as a whole and into negotiating the buying of the building were different. We all feel we have some kind of stake in the building but our perception of that stake varies. However, if we stop there all we've got is conflict and any resolution of the problems in front of us can only come at the expense of whatever minority loses out at some future vote. (...) What is our common ground? (...) We have always tried to get a consensus on all really important issues even if it meant putting off a decision for a while. Nobody has wanted to operate from personal power but rather we have wanted to be guided by the "rightness" of a proposed solution which everyone could agree upon.' It will be interesting to see how this spirit will have influenced the organizing efforts in Nusquama a couple of years from now.

Friendly non-Christians interested in the new church orientation towards total service in the neighbourhood have reacted positively to the invitation to be part of the parish councils, 'to ensure our authenticity', as the letter said. Non-believers is a term that in most cases doesn't completely do justice to their convictions. Those who have been invited are all committed people, certainly involved in a sincere search that goes beyond their own well-being and reaches out to the neighbourhood. In certain cases the parish is amazed that they would go as far as they have gone because they don't always see the same generosity in the parish. One has spoken a lot in publications about the post-Christian era. One of the positive results might be the fact that these so-called non-Christians don't feel the need constantly to criticize the Church or to emphasize their own freedom from 'sectarian attitudes' but are frankly interested in any positive commitment in the neighbourhood and in the city. Like in many places in America, Jewish people are working closely together on all levels with the church in many situations, and in Nusquama it is less and less rare to find Christians in the synagogues or at special feasts. Rabbis teach Old Testament theology at courses for continuing education. I met one Rabbi who teaches in Jewish groups chants he had learnt in a church; the chants have this particularity that they repeat the same words over and over again and are continued as long as possible until their ultimate truth penetrates deep down into the people present. He thinks it is a way of singing and 'tasting' the Divine that fits very well into the Hassidic tradition.

Each year a city-wide gathering is held in Center Park. Not everybody likes it with all the noise, the mixture of all kinds of people, the suffocating atmosphere of the crowd, the evangelistic style, the long talks and sermons, the prayers that never end and the fatigue of sitting on the ground in the midst of all those other bodies. But at least it is a totally ecumenical festival where all the gifts of the people are shared together, all the religious traditions are brought in, all spiritual families are honoured and all kinds of religious music are blended. At the end there is half an hour of silence. Many people come only for this part. I heard about busloads of people who travel hundreds of miles to be part of this silence. The topic that was presented for discussion has never totally come across because the people need more than half an hour to find where their group is gathered, to introduce themselves, to overcome the language barriers, to wait until the first one dares to speak, and then it is already time to stop and to join the next activity. But they come every year because they know that after all the talking, the organ concerts, the market for Christian commitments, the choir rehearsals, the Gregorian chant of the monks, the Gospel singers, the peace declarations, the blessings, the walking from one place to another, the gags, there will be that silence. It is as a matter of fact an incredible experience to see thousands of people sitting, standing, lying, kneeling, without doing anything. They seem to be staring at an invisible point or at someone who is holding seven stars in his right hand or to be listening to an inaudible sound like the rippling of a creek or the sound of a breeze or to be waiting for an imminent surprise as if they were the three wise men wandering in Jerusalem. Many don't like it when the silence is finally broken by some blaring trumpet on the podium. It is time to take the train if you can get in with those crowds, it is again time to climb and to descend, to deepen and to share, a time to look for work and a time to protest, to struggle for justice and to put on new wings, a time of sacrifices and a time of compassion, a time to suffer, a time to rise again.

An invisible structure of pastoral care
Spiritually, the church in Nusquama has rediscovered an old monastic system according to which every member regularly has the opportunity to sit down for an hour of

silence, rest and personal sharing with one of the older members who have been trained for this ministry. It is an effort that demands much time and energy but it has been chosen as an essential initiative for personal formation, prayerful listening and constant awakening of the vocation to which each one is called. A certain regularity in these visits is considered important. People don't choose their 'brother' or 'sister' but they are consulted before the decision to enter into this spiritual alliance is made. The rhythm of regularity is different and varies between once a week and once a month. The style varies as well: a sharing of daily events and projects for the future over a glass of wine; a conversation that resembles a confession of sins; a long process of spiritual deepening; counselling what books could be read or which longer retreat would be advisable. People like it. They say that it is very refreshing to be listened to and to speak in a more intimate setting about what weighs upon them. There is no reciprocity, in the sense that the listener does not speak about him – or herself. The listener and his or her visitor don't speak about the contents of their personal sharing outside of the context of this weekly or monthly hour. Nobody else knows to whom a parishioner goes but everybody knows that the listeners go to others who will listen to them. A network is built up that remains invisible but that sustains the whole spiritual building up of the church. These conversations don't replace sacramental confession, which should be accomplished in the presence of the priest, but they are very helpful in preparing the ground for a confession that renews the whole person. In Nusquama they have given up group sharing because of the complex situations that arose out of that. This formula demands of course a lot of commitment of each person; a built-in flexibility allows, however, the style of the conversation to be adapted to whatever level seems appropriate to the actual situation of the visitor on the day of his or her visit. It is striking that especially old people have been chosen, sometimes as a couple, to fulfil this ministry. Although it is a discipline for them not to speak themselves – they train for this in the preparation courses – they marvel at being part of this ministry.

Over the past years inter-American solidarity has become a clear challenge for many Christians. There were political reasons for this attention given to Latin America because of the US Government's struggle against liberation movements. But in many places a sense of complementarity was growing as well; especially in the Church, North Americans felt they needed the gifts of Latin-Americans. While the Latin-American emphasis on the preferential option for the poor and on the struggle for justice is more and more accepted as an essential component of Christian life and of the life of the Church, North Americans were looking for a rediscovery of the dimension of contemplation. Words like 'spirituality', 'deepening', 'retreat' could be found across the spectrum of spiritual families. But often one sensed in it a rebirth of quietism. In the big suburban retreat houses, in the shade of life tree oaks, in the purity of countryside woods, in long walks along desert beaches, people felt they could breathe again but then, sitting still on the floor at the end of the day, they yawned. In a culture in which the outside world was faraway or harsh or threatening, in a social environment in which the me-values were more easily cherished than the values of the other, not a few people retired, turned inwards and placed their hope in an inner quietness by sitting still waiting for the emergence of an unattainable inner peace to calm the clamour of the world and the cacophony of inner contradictions. But the attentiveness to the Latin-American scene has turned this self-centredness around.

I see an example of this in the 'justice-retreats' in Nusquama. Families in poor areas open their homes to people who are willing to make such a retreat. On a brochure I read some of the questions that have to be addressed during such a time of reflection: 'How can Christian communities become visible signs of reconcili-

156

ation amidst the painful divisions in the human family? How do the roots of our Christian faith challenge our lives to overcome hatred in ourselves and to work for justice among all peoples? How can we commit ourselves as Christians to become agents of justice, of communion, of sharing for all humanity? How can we prepare ourselves to live our lives so that no person is victim of another? In your own situation, in order to abolish hatred and injustice, will you be a bearer of reconciliation in the divisions of the Christian family, and in those which tear apart the human family? How can we begin together?' One of the interesting elements of this questionnaire is the recurrent 'we'. Those who make this retreat are invited to walk around in the neighbourhood, to take part every evening in local community meetings, to expose oneself to the needs of the area, to live with the family and to address these questions in quiet morning hours.

Everywhere I went I noticed the link made between the local church and community organization. People are even surprised that I am surprised about it! They say that it is normal to have on the parish council a certain number of people who are community organizers, independent yet working closely with the parishioners. In the seventies and early eighties prayer, parish and church programmes on the one hand and justice issues, neighbourhood versus city concerns and the questioning of national policies on the other were so estranged one from another that people had to choose between them. It seems that the growing interest in the Latin-American experience as well as the fact that down there Christians place all their hope in the Church, seeing it as the place for social justice par excellence, has helped to overcome this dichotomy. It started with small peace and justice groups tolerated on the fringe of the parish but viewed with distrust. Fortunately the 'activists', as they were called, did not have an attitude of political moralism by which the others would have felt judged and excluded or considered as lesser Christians who had not yet attained the

157

fullness of adult faith. On the contrary, they had been wise enough to integrate gradually many other components of parish life. To give an example, they spent as much time in church as the sacristan. They had even extended certain Masses by a night of prayer during which one after the other would intercede for one hour, praying for situations of extreme tension because of unrest in the city or painful international events. The parishioners had also learned that these people cared for the people in the neighbourhood. So they hadn't any more the fear of getting involved in a kind of power game. Their own concerns seemed to have been placed in the wider context of the real life of the whole community and all the aspects of the life of the people. In one or two cases certain events had particularly united the people who previously had been opponents and who didn't talk much together.

In one church it concerned the issue if transients would be allowed to sit in the church during the day. It seems that a long discussion was necessary before the parish council decided to open up the pews on both sides of the church, to install some bathrooms and showers and to organize a welcome in the basement for coffee, games and company. Some abandoned buildings in the area had been repaired and renovated by the parishioners as shelters for the transients. They looked like hotels, with ladies from the parish at the entrance. They belonged to an organization called 'Ladies of Hope'. Elsewhere, the question had been asked if the church could become a public sanctuary. There is a difference between private and public sanctuary. Private means you house refugees who escaped their country for political reasons but you do it quietly, you don't let anybody know about it which is just as illegal as public sanctuary. The feeling in this parish was that the reason for the refugees coming to the United States was as important to deal with as caring for them. Without the prophetic dimension, they said, you are just allowing a very repressive regime to continue, to victimize and terrorize people. A family of six lives in the church. The pastor with whom I spoke said 'When you measure the cost of us maybe losing our non-profit status, it is such a pitifully passive sacrifice compared to what they're sacrificing'. They are now reflecting upon possibilities of extending this hospitality to refugees, asking the parishioners to share their life with them.

Turn your building into a village
I visit a young couple. They are just married and, although they were rather middle-class in background, they wanted to start their life together with an option somehow the opposite of what people yearn for in general. Rather than to look for the nicest apartment they could imagine – with a tree, sufficient outside lighting, a lively neighbourhood with young adults around, a nice view of the city – they had decided to live in a Dominican neighbourhood, certainly not the poorest in the city but a lower-class one, with people recently arrived, mainly undocumented and all speaking Spanish, a language they are now learning actively. It seems the neighbours are surprised and even suspect them of living in that area in order to save money before moving out again. The couple do not yet know what the future will bring but they found it necessary for themselves to live out a symbol of sharing among other people, especially among those who are disadvantaged in comparison with the suburban world where they come from.

That evening the Dean invited me to a Greek restaurant next to the cathedral. From under his plate he took a napkin with the Odyssey itinerary printed on it. We were talking architecture. With a few lines he sketched the outline of his cathedral, the cathedral grounds, the park, the high-rise buildings in the immediate vicinity used by hospitals and schools and the blighted area in the distance. Pushing with an elegant gesture the long silver hair hanging over his eyes to a different part of his head so as better to appreciate the accuracy of his sketch, he announced a preliminary remark

that would soon follow, immediately after we had finished
our glasses filled to the brim with sweet *samos*. His point
was, summarized in a few words, that in the city's present
financial crisis and in the midst of the exodus led by
corporations into exurbia, we should set up at the very
centre of the city a sign of hope, of new beginning, of
enthusiasm by building again. We don't build any more
with generosity, with magnificence; rather we have to fill up
our churches with all kinds of extraneous organizations that
rent the space for an evening or a day without sharing its
beliefs and mysteries. We should be building again like the
Pharaohs in Egypt. The Church should not yield to the
general irresponsibility towards the city but start again to
become the heart of the city.

I reacted by saying that I was afraid the Church would
then build signs of power, wealth and domination rather
than hopeful signs of presence and closeness. Why would
you take out of funds that could be used otherwise
tremendous amounts of money just to erect a sign without
knowing how the edifices can be filled? But he had all the
answers. First of all, the money was not with no strings
attached; it had to be used for building, it said so in the will.
Secondly, he was only speaking about the towers. 'There
are no towers in my cathedral.' He drew immense neo-
Gothic towers, and in the towers small lines dividing them
up into floors and into apartments, linking them with small
oval lines at the spots where balconies with flowers on the
railing could emerge. He calculated the number of poor
people who could live there; they would all belong to the
category of people who by themselves would never make it
out of their ghetto. In the evening the towers would sparkle
with all the lights on in the rooms and add to the evening
luminosity of Nusquama.

I found the idea incredible. I know there is one apartment
in the towers of Notre-Dame of Paris. Writers have
imagined bell-ringers living in cathedral towers. I myself
have lived in a cathedral rectory in Italy built next to the

cathedral. Walking from my room on the third floor along the loggia to one of the cathedral's windows I could follow the unfolding of the liturgy downstairs. But now, at this restaurant table, we were in imagination socializing all this. If we took all the towers of Nusquama – two, three thousand? – of all the denominations that have sprung up in this Bible belt, how many apartments could we build? The napkin again .... Three thousand towers with fifty units each would make one hundred and fifty thousand units for three hundred thousand people or more.... It would be easy to raise money for such a fantastic idea and to get subventions, because the Church would have made an essential contribution to the housing shortage in Nusquama. Maybe by doing this they would even give an example to individual Christians, leading them to make an inventory of all the empty places they can find in their secondary residences, hangars, underoccupied apartments, superfluous office space and help them to share. A lot of life would come back to the church, the parish grounds, the elementary school; hopefully, one of the results would be full churches. The bellringers would finish work at 9pm and not start before 8am. The carillon melodies would be chosen according to the wishes of the tower people. One condition for living in the tower would be some involvement in the welcome at the entrance of the church. Nobody would enter without seeing lots of mothers with their children in and around the 'cry room' in the front of the church. Some of them would explain to visitors all the exciting things that had happened to the life of the Church in Nusquama.

We talked and saw so many perspectives for this community living in and around the church, with possibilities for a daily prayer together, a special presence in the neighbourhood, mutual assistance. And we were staring at the odyssey the Church would undertake from this table to high-rise church towers for the poor and churches overflowing with people to magnificent liturgies celebrated by the people one with another and shared with all the other poor

161

in the area. Is this the second or the third glass? I asked.

In most of the rectories where I stayed I lost a lot of time every day simply by having to walk from my bedroom through one or two antechambers to the end of the apartment and then through the corridors, into the elevator, and down to the dining room. I remember how I often stumbled in corridors over all the possessions that had been stocked there as a spillover from the other priests' apartments. They have come to the rectory as gifts and donations from overzealous faithful or because of the priests' hobbies that can include electronics, non-Western chasubles, sporting goods, African sculpture or – more commonly – books. In Nusquama, some priests have taken a sabbatical to proceed with an 'aggiornamento' of the places they live in. In extreme cases, for instance, in houses where a swimming pool belonged to the Church property, they decided to remove them. It is true that the priests of that particular parish had never found the time to jump into the swimming pool but they had found that it hurt the image of their ascetic life, which means a life of renunciation. Taking part one day in a discussion about this whole subject, I found it hard to accept the fact that the priests had to simplify their lives, almost punishing themselves, while the rest of the neighbourhood was swimming in its wealth and still found it necessary to criticize the priests who live as guests in the diocesan rectories and can be called away on short notice by a bishop and placed in a completely different area. On the other hand, I emphasized that simplicity undoubtedly had its own charm, that the whole minimal house decoration was becoming more and more in, that certain electronic instruments could be easily hidden behind curtains and inside of closets, that the real value of simplification would have to be found in sharing with others and especially the poor, for instance with those who had no home at all. Would it be possible, I asked, to give away a whole floor of the rectory to some refugees on one side of the house with a separate entrance? Would it not also give a feeling of community which seems important for the life of priests who have an incredibly dense ministry twelve to twenty hours a day?

The seven task forces in each parish

In Nusquama each parish council is composed of twenty-one members like the Carmelite monasteries. Apparently, even here church life can't function without structures and some uniformity. They try to have young people as well on the council, even children. The twenty-one members are divided among seven task forces in which they work in teams of three. Each task force centres on one of the Beatitudes. The preferential option for the poor is evident in the first one. Being a team of three doesn't mean that they have to do all the work themselves but that they are attentive to the poor, and look at the parish, the sermons, the liturgy, the parish activities through the eyes of the poor and imagine how the church itself could become poor and a place where the poor feel at home and are invited to the banquet of the Kingdom. They are guardians who make sure that the poor are always first. As a matter of fact they have been chosen themselves from among the poorest of the poor. Quite naturally the team doesn't work out statements or discuss problems of poverty in general but finds facts and imagines concrete ministries to be fulfilled by the parishioners. The cask of the Danaids, the endless well of poverty in their society is such a constant challenge for them that they often have brought up in the parish council the question of how to deal with their powerlessness to answer all the human needs: should we really become a stronghold for the poor? Is that the right direction? A universally available social agency full of good intentions? Or, more fundamentally, a place where they are welcomed, where we suffer with them in poverty of spirit, sharing what we can, pointing towards God who in our common poverty is our only security?

A second team works with the mourning, the sick, the

elderly. The team of the Beatitude of the meek works for reconciliation. It is healthy that regularly conflicts arise. Here is a team that reminds people all the time about the basic mission of reconciliation, and the pressing need of living this first among ourselves before speaking out about peace to others. This team also has in its job description the task of opening windows, doors and hearts to others in the neighbourhood, especially to non-Christians. The Nusquama parish knows the temptation of becoming a self-contained entity that people would take for the real world, while it is only a place where one retires for prayer like the mountain was for Jesus, a community of people who renew themselves and one another in the joy of the Resurrection, a space where something of the Beatitudes becomes visible and a starting-point for people to root their pilgrimage before going out to encounter the world. The team is attentive to non-Christians, inviting them to give their vision of the Church. They don't see non-believers as souls to be conquered or bodies to be incorporated but as people who, like all human beings, carry around at the heart of their existence a profound mystery out of which could spring forth intuitions the Church needs in order to become authentic.

The team in charge of purity – purity of heart, said Kierkegaard, is the will to do the one necessary thing – is called to find ways to embellish life, to infuse the daily greyness with the grass-green colour of hope, the human darkness with the rainbow colours of faith and love. Artists from the neighbourhood play an important role in the parish. They paint murals, redecorate the choir space at the church, invent every week a new setting as we do in our own houses or in the way we dress up for special occasions. Beauty in a church, especially in the city, is like flowers in a world of concrete, a garden amidst abandoned houses, like a sweet breeze after days of oppressive heat, a breath of new life in the contemplation of a child and a sign that there is more in these few years we live on earth than economics.

This team is also in charge of faith in the church. They mean by purity in this context that somehow the totality of Christ has to be kept as a treasure, even if the people carry Him in earthen vessels and go through times in which fluctuations of doubt, unbelief and inner obscurity seem to extirpate the purity and spontaneity of our surrender to His cross and resurrection. Some people have to keep up the treasure of faith high above the destructive revolt and the shrinking of our souls. As a symbol they bring into the services high above themselves the Scriptures, the bread and the wine and an icon of Christ so that people learn again and again to admire and to marvel about what the whole tradition of the Church has given us.

The justice team is in charge of advocacy for the poor, community organization, demonstrations, contacts with local institutions as well as of justice among the people who belong to the Church in Nusquama as a whole. Their efforts over the past years have been very much orientated towards effective ways of sharing between suburban and urban churches. The merciful are in charge of financing. The church has thought that only those penetrated by compassion could handle money, the root of all evil, as Saint Paul says. Only they are able to give away freely and to be surprised when funds come in again. They don't keep money, it goes from their left to their right hand and never remains trapped in savings accounts. The last team focuses on other countries, especially places where oppressed or persecuted people live. Often the council meetings start with their reports about what is going on in Namibia or Cambodia or Lebanon. It is not a matter of intellectual discussion or sentimental justification of their guilt feelings; only exceptionally they would publish a statement as a cry that can no longer be repressed. Essentially it is a matter of bearing others' burdens, offering and entrusting them to Christ and then of waiting for gestures, actions, initiatives that can be undertaken.

Other tasks are shared all together, for instance the

liturgy, which is considered to be the heart of their life together.

Every parishioner has a ministry, a specific one in which he or she has been confirmed for one year or for a longer period of time. One of the results is that the priest's ministry becomes one among all the other ministries, and that he is more an enabler, a helper to people who are struggling in the ministry that is theirs. The lady from India who is married to a scientist cooks meals for the homeless. The chairman of a local bank helps the custodian to clean up the church on Saturday evening and all day Sunday. Cambodian immigrants preach sometimes, in their own language. The Koreans, the Vietnamese and the English-speaking join for Mass, using their languages and a fourth one because of the communion with other peoples living elsewhere in the world. In seven years they go through all the languages of the world, and they start again with the first letter of the alphabet (Abyssinian language). A harpist plays away the sadness of the burdened. Several people have a monthly prayer list and meet for intercession time. Children mime the Sunday gospel. Some women learn to sing antiphons. A man who in his youth felt abandoned by his parents is named good shepherd; he has to care for all the people who don't feel invited, honoured, taken seriously, who feel humiliated by the priest or the secretary, who are never visited by anybody, never greeted on the streets, never asked for anything. A young woman who stuttered for some deep psychological reasons speaks in tongues at every prayer meeting. A lady who is chronically ill receives people and children for confidential conversations and spiritual help. A shopping-bag lady who directs day after day the traffic on the corner of Church Avenue is in charge of hand-outs and refreshments (beware when you refuse a second cup of coffee). Unknown artists exhibit their works in the basement of the church, and the bankers of the parish draw their clientèle there to look and to buy. A dancer dances psalms of David. Some painters cover the apse with hieratic

166

graffiti. Senior citizens give 'Life and Faith seminars' to young people and students. A pilot flies good news from elsewhere home. A disabled priest at the hospital has the SOS line twenty-four hours a day. A policeman repairs broken boilers in the co-ops in his free time. The parish council has told the politician to do his job well, and nothing else, and to do it as a ministry of compassion. A lady is allowed to take her cats to church. A man who says he is not able to do anything, and who had wept in admitting it, has been named chairman of the parish council. The choirs take a lot of people as well as the rock-group and the blues ensemble. A woman writes short stories and poems for the social evenings. Her husband calligraphs Bibles given to newlyweds. The mentally ill from Hartley House are driven in on Saturdays for games, copious dinners and singing because the others like to have them around. Bingo money is invested in carnival preparation. There is a large visitors' group to visit prisoners, shut-ins, people in the hospitals, places of hope in the city, ex-Christians, churches in other cities. At the Bible school the gospel is explained out of the mouths of babes and sucklings. The restaurant owner brings in food surpluses. And whoever has for the moment nothing to do knows that their essential ministry is to suffer with the suffering and to be joyful with those in joy.

What was the most fundamental thing I learned during the time I spent in Nusquama? All the new initiatives, the new structures? The proof that the Church can go further than its conformity with society around it by radicalizing its witness? The search for reconciliation seen as the only basis from which everything else flows? The energy of people of all generations enthusiastic about the Church's ministry? The impression that church life provoked the same amazement as the mobilization of the young in the sixties or the announcement of Vatican II among Christians? An old institution coming to life, spreading abundant life all around? The victory over sectarianism and openness to the arts, to new life styles, to the technological age? Although it

167

sounds almost too simple to be true, in Nusquama I was impressed by the joy of the people. The word church for them is no longer synonymous with boredom but with life, and with the heart of life. Elsewhere one meets so many wrinkled faces visibly worrying about how things will continue in the future, with the financial collapse, the lack of vocations, the secularization, the neo-paganism in society, and so forth. Here I found a gladness made up of gratitude and inner creativity that contents itself with knowing all that one receives together with the others in the communion of the Church: the awe of God, the grace of Christ, the imagination of the Holy Spirit, the Word, the Eucharist, the other sacraments, an aim for our lives, a hope for every person, the call to commitment, the world of prayer and silence, the understanding of suffering, the closeness to the life of the exploited and the poor, gentleness and sympathy, simplicity and mercy, the sense of universality, the vision of eternal life....

About Taizé by Brother John

Why would a small group of "ecumenical monks" undertake a pilgrimage of peace and reconciliation across North America, visiting over thirty cities in the course of a year and a half? To answer that question, it is necessary to understand a little more about both the calling of our community and the roots of biblical faith.

Many people know the Taizé Community as an ecumenical monastic community, living since 1940 in a small village in eastern France. At that time our founder and prior, Brother Roger, came and settled in Taizé to offer a haven to political refugees and to form, with others, a "parable of community," an existential sign of Christ's love in a world torn apart by divisions. The life of the brothers, from the beginning, was centered on prayer, work, and hospitality. They strove to be attentive to the signs of the times, working after the war, for example, with German prisoners and taking in a group of children orphaned by the war. In time, the community became known both for its worship and as a center of prayer and reflection on ways of overcoming the divisions among Christians. Finally, in the 1960s searching young adults began coming to Taizé. Numbers continued to increase, and today thousands arrive each week, especially in the summer. During the week-long meetings run by the community throughout the year, they explore the sources of their faith.

Because of our community's commitment to reconciliation, we have never wanted to create a "movement" of our own, searching instead for ways of helping people become more involved in their own local situation. Taizé never has seen itself as a self-centered, all-inclusive reality; from the beginning brothers went out to live in small groups on different continents. They went not to try to solve people's problems for them, but in order to be simple "signs of Christ's presence and hearers of joy" *(Rule of Taizé),* to live, work, and pray in the midst of tensions and divisions. Today, for example, brothers live in Bangladesh, Calcutta, Kenya, Brazil, Japan, and Korea as well as New York City.

Since 1978, a small group of brothers has been living in a poor neighborhood on Manhattan's West Side known as "Hell's Kitchen." Along with some other people, the brothers squatted an almost abandoned tenement building. After a lot of work and years of negotiation, they were able to form a cooperative and to acquire the building from the City of New York.

The first years of the community's presence in New York were centered on local involvement. The brothers have worked—and still work—in various neighborhood programs for the elderly, the homeless, etc. Another brother works at the Center for Seafarer's Rights of Seaman's Church Institute, which tries to respond to the growing exploitation of those who work on the world's ships, especially in the booming cruise industry. In 1980 and 1981, Taizé organized several large meetings in New York and other East Coast cities, in Montreal and Toronto. These were weekends of sharing between Christians of different backgrounds along the lines of the gatherings which have been taking place in European cities for some time now.

Then, in December 1982, Brother Roger went to Lebanon. After meeting and praying with Christians and Muslims, he decided to launch a worldwide pilgrimage of peace and reconciliation, lasting several years at least and involving meetings and visits between Christians and with all people of good will on every continent.

Why a pilgrimage? Pilgrimages are of course an aspect of many religions, but in the Bible they take on a significance far beyond that of merely journeying to a holy place. The first pilgrim we meet in the Bible is Abraham, the father of God's people; God calls him to set out into the unknown, armed only with faith (Genesis 12:1-4; cf. Hebrews 11:8-10). The Exodus, the core of Israel's faith, is also a story of pilgrimage; centuries later, when the people are deported to Babylon, prophets arise to announce the "good news" of a new Exodus back to the promised land and the holy city (e.g., Isaiah 43:16-21). Jesus is likewise a pilgrim; he has no place to lay his head (Luke 9:58) and comes to show us the way to God and to one another. Every believer is called to leave everything behind and to set out in Jesus' footsteps (Mark 1:16-20; Matthew 16:24-26) as an "ambassador of reconciliation" (cf. 2 Corinthians 5:20).

The notion of pilgrimage is thus an extremely rich one for deepening our understanding of the gospel. It helps us better to grasp the dimension of the provisional, of finding security in God alone and of not settling down in the illusory comforts and values society offers us. It also provides a framework for living out the double dimension of communion or reconciliation that is at the very heart of the gospel. God has reconciled us to the Divine Self in Christ (2 Corinthians 5:18-19), and as a consequence all the barriers which once separated us have fallen, "there is neither Jew nor Greek, slave nor free, male nor female" (Galatians 3:28). Our journey to God and in God's company thus becomes simultaneously a pilgrimage toward one another, leading us beyond all the divisions that normally keep us apart.

The call to a worldwide pilgrimage of peace and reconciliation thus became for us living in New York the beginning of a new stage in our presence in North America. We saw it as a call to go and join Christians throughout Canada and the United States, to share their lives for a while and to worship with them, to discover their sufferings and their hopes. At the same time, other brothers are undertaking similar pilgrimages on other continents. As a text written a few years ago in Taizé puts it: "When divisions and rivalries bring things to a standstill, nothing is more important than setting out to visit and listen to one another, and to celebrate the paschal mystery together."

Most of the pilgrimages have taken the form of a weekend sponsored by a group of churches or Christians in a town. They are all organized locally, with some help from us, and each has its own character. A typical framework would be as follows: People arrive on Friday evening to a central site for registration and a worship service centered around the cross. Sometimes small-group discussions bring people together to discover the sufferings that they are particularly concerned with and would like to share with others and bring to Christ.

The worship is very meditative in style. We use the repetitive chants developed in Taizé over the past few years which are becoming more and more familiar to North Americans. The service includes a long litany where everyone's intentions are mentioned and rhythmed by a response such as *Kyrie eleison* (Lord, have mercy). A prayer around the cross follows, an opportunity for people to go up and pray for a few moments around an icon of the cross we always bring with us on our pilgrimage as a sign that Christ is at the center. This prayer around the cross is a concrete gesture of bringing one's sufferings and laying them at Jesus' feet. Somehow in this litany and prayer I always have the overwhelming impression that all humanity's sufferings are being expressed and taken up into the heart of God.

Saturday morning is generally a quiet time. Following a morning prayer there is often Bible study on a topic such as "the roots of peace," then a period of silent reflection and/or small-group discussions. After noon prayer and lunch, participants are often sent out to "places of suffering and hope" in the area—places where people are attempting to deal with various kinds of social problems and human suffering. Participants have thus visited soup kitchens, shelters for the homeless, people who work with alcoholics and drug addicts, others active in the peace movement, and so on. It is an experience of listening, and a way of discovering things happening right in your own home town that you are usually unaware of. The "places of hope" are discovered and chosen by the local group preparing the meeting, and setting up this part of the meeting has always been a powerful experience for those concerned. In one small town in Iowa, for example, the person responsible for this was unsure he could find any such places. After searching for a while he came up with over fifty, many more than were needed! There is a call to use our imagination. In one town, one place of hope was that of an elderly woman who spent time painting portraits of all the unsung heroes of that town and had created an art gallery in her own home for them.

At the end of the afternoon, people return to a central place and share stories of their discoveries during the afternoon. After a festive meal, the day closes with a prayer service centered around the resurrection. Usually this matches the mood of the participants; the sharing of sufferings, the times of quiet reflection and the discovery of new initiatives often cause new hope mysteriously to spring up. The service concludes with a reading of the gospel of the resurrection while everyone holds a lighted candle. The next day, Sunday, the people are urged to return to their local congregations to share something of what they have seen and heard.

In Ann Arbor, the weekend was an initiative of campus ministers of the University of Michigan. During the pilgrimage we journeyed from church to church, including black and white Baptist churches, a Roman Catholic parish, and a Christian Reformed congregation. In Madison, Wisconsin, our pilgrimage coincided with the Week for Christian Unity. We prayed every day for a week in two different churches, going all the way from a black Baptist congregation to an Eastern Orthodox parish. Many local people joined us day after day, and it was a brand-new experience of discovering one another's traditions and the common underlying unity.

A particularly striking experience for us was our pilgrimage on the Gaspe peninsula in eastern Quebec province. It had been well prepared by a pastoral team that had visited parishes in many different villages. As we traveled from village to village for a time of prayer and sharing, our coming seemed to make visible and to celebrate what the people had already been reflecting on; as in the gospel parable, we had the privilege of harvesting the fruits that others had sown. In the town of Restigouche, we visited the Micmac Indian reserve. The prayer service in the church there was packed, and many whites came over from nearby New Brunswick. After the prayer, the native people invited everyone for a small celebration, during which the children danced traditional dances. We were told that such an evening with native people and whites together was an extremely rare occurrence, "a kind of miracle," one person said.

Our own role in all these events has been more than anything else that of a catalyst. We provide the occasion for people to come together outside of their customary circle of friends and acquaintances, in a context of worship and listening; the Spirit does the rest. This pilgrimage has reinforced our conviction that God has provided people with all the necessary gifts to be a leaven of peace and justice in the world. There are many hopeful signs in the church of Jesus Christ; what is most urgent is creating links between these many different realities that already exist. For Christians the roots of peace lie in the conviction of a common belonging—we belong to Christ and to God (1 Corinthians 3:23), and we are members of one another (Romans 12:5). When we express this common belonging, our suffering is transfigured into joy and hope. That has been our deepest discovery in the course of our time "on pilgrimage"; we have seen that reconciliation is possible only if we realize that we need one another in order to be faithful to Jesus. If we open our hearts to others who bear the name of Christ like us, even a small group of women and men can change the course of history by transforming disillusionment and resignation into a dynamic hope.